RIVER OF FIRE:

Incidents in the Life of a Woman Deputy Sheriff

My Beloved Mother Story,
Also A Woman of God
1/11/2017

RIVER OF FIRE:

Incidents in the Life of a Woman Deputy Sheriff

by

Maria Pereira

with

A. Myrna Nurse, PhD

iUniverse, Inc.

New York   Bloomington

River of Fire
Incidents in the Life of a Woman Deputy Sheriff

iUniverse books may be ordered through booksellers or by contacting:

iUniverse
1663 Liberty Drive
Bloomington, IN 47403
www.iuniverse.com
1-800-Authors (1-800-288-4677)

ISBN: 978-1-4401-4840-8 (pbk)
ISBN: 978-1-4401-4841-5 (dj)
ISBN: 978-1-4401-4842-2 (ebk)

Printed in the United States of America

iUniverse rev. date: 6/29/2009

God, the Silversmith, burns away the dross,
refining the silver and gold
so that we may emerge
bright and shining.

— Malachi 3.3-4 (paraphrased)

Contents

PREFACE

Life in the U.S. for minority immigrant women poses challenges that women who are born here will never encounter. Without attempting to hierarchize discrimination or pain, undoubtedly only a minority immigrant woman knows what it's like to experience prejudice as a woman, an immigrant, and a minority. When these factors are added to the reality that she may already be educated, as many women from the Caribbean and Latin America, India, Africa, and the Asiatic countries are, her education may not be an asset but a liability. Other demographic factors may include age, religion, and sexuality, which make being an immigrant woman who simply wants to provide a decent life for herself and her children no simple task.

After sharing briefly with Myrna some of her experiences in America, Maria and Myrna found that they shared some commonalities and realized that developing Maria's trials and triumphs into an inspirational narrative was doable. Myrna's interest in Maria's story was sparked by Maria's former career as a deputy sheriff, as one of Myrna's 1999 doctoral dissertation's focuses was on women and the U.S. prison industrial complex. However, more compellingly was that both are immigrants from Trinidad and Tobago. The women first met in 2001 when Myrna was conducting post-doctoral research on the growth of the steelband movement in the U.S., and Maria—a life-long friend of Dr. Elliot Mannette of Morgantown, West Virginia—contributed a vignette in relation to Mannette's story. Now, the authors in collaboration present Maria's experiences that describe a woman who, with tenacity and courage, pursued her dream of being in law enforcement at an age when many people are considering retirement.

Spiritually, they both hold a deep, abiding faith in God, the Source of all things. They both accept that God's Son Jesus Christ has completed a miraculous, though mysterious, work that is necessary to all people's salvation. Socially, they both love steelband music and appreciate the spirit of Carnival from which steelband music has emerged, despite Carnival being antithetical to Christianity. They both agree that it is only a loving God who could bring together an Indian woman and a multiracial black one to say in one voice that race is a social construction, the evils of racism one day will cease to strangle human relationships, and women will continue to reach across the racial divide to pray and work together.

Without apologizing for the often low tenor of Maria's overall story, they prefer that the reader see past this toward appreciating the only purpose of the story: to reaffirm that after we've been through the fire, we do emerge shining like pure gold. The "river of fire" that began with Shadrach, Meshach, and Abednego and flowed ferociously throughout the subsequent ages in its attempt to lick greedily its victims has again been unsuccessful. Maria's story is not one of defeat but rather of how she has turned her adversity into a river of life. She and Myrna wish it to be seen as the way in which she faced her demons during the darkest moment of her life and prevailed. She followed her conscience, kindled by her new faith, uncompromisingly. Indeed, she has walked through the "valley of the shadow of death" and now fears no evil.

Lastly, the authors iterate that though everyone generally expects a story to have a happy or triumphant ending, sometimes victory is in the waiting. In regard to one's faith, waiting in turn inculcates growth in confidence that the Alpha and Omega are always already in control, from their first word-sound, "Let there be light," to their final, triumphant "Amen!"

CHAPTER 1 — RIVERS OF LIFE

My journey toward becoming a deputy sheriff of Atlanta's Fulton County Sheriff Department began in the far outskirts of the flat Caroni Plains, home of many Indo-Trinidadians. While I was glad to immigrate to the U.S., now that I'm retired and have plenty time on my hands to look back upon my life, I'm pestered with one question. Why was my career aborted during the last term of my career? Some days, the sharp, stabbing pain of my miscarriage of justice left me staggering, and the only thing I could do to stop myself from hemorrhaging like the woman in the book of St. Marks was to reach out and touch his garment with my streams of prayers. Similarly to her, my issue was healed, even though it took me a while to recognize how the healing came. Until then, many mornings I awoke demanding to know what I'd done wrong. I took to scratching around in memory of Ma's stories of our ancestral East Indian mothers who survived through thick and thin to finally come to the decision that I'd done nothing fundamentally wrong on my job, only that I could have done some things differently.

It took me as long as it did to so conclude because of the layers of complexities I had to unveil, and not it was not because I was slow. Ma started to call me slow after one of my elementary school teachers wrote on my report card, "Maria is a bright girl but tends to be slow sometimes." Ma took to teasing me that I was so slow in some things that I flowed backward, like the time—only once, but who really knows?—the Indus River flowed backward. Ma used to tell me stories of India as we went through our daily chores. Sometimes, I listened to every word. Other times, I just stopped listening and let my imagination go back to the places she used to describe as if she were born there. She wasn't and probably got those stories second-hand from her mother-in-law, Granma, who died before I was born. (Ma was Venezuelan and light-skinned but knew things about India that she must have learned from my father's side of the family; he was a dark-skinned Indian, like his mother. I inherited my darker skin from him.)

You should know that Ma wasn't educated according to today's standard. Yet, she knew the names of India's two main rivers, the Indus and the Ganges, and described them like she'd sat or played on their banks and inhaled their fragrant sprays, and as if human progress did nothing to pollute their waters. Only once she mentioned Portugal, linking it to the part of India my ancestral Indian mothers came from that was settled by the Portuguese. She wasn't bitter about those Portuguese colonizers who came, saw, and conquered because people's behavior was just like rivers—confined and unconfined, limited and limitless, giving life and taking life.

Back then, I didn't know why rivers held their mystical power over her when she couldn't even tell me the part of India my father's mothers came from or which river gave them life, Indus or Ganges. The best I made of all her talk about rivers was that she appreciated access to clean water and wasn't too happy with our Hindu neighbors who monopolized the banks of the Caroni River with their cremation rituals. She grumbled—in agreement with our fellow Trinidadians—that access to the river was for everyone who had as much right to enjoy it before it entered the saline marshes of the Caroni Swamp, whose mouth kissed the Gulf of Paria that eventually mingled with the Caribbean Sea and the Atlantic Ocean.

I used to get lost in her descriptions of all the flowing and swirling waters that flowed around, over, and beneath obstacles to arrive in oceans. Rivers and oceans that rose invisibly to dance in the clouds until they returned to the earth in gentle taps. Or, if their heavy footsteps collided, in protest of the violent collisions, they took their vengeance back to earth as monsoons, typhoons, cyclones, mud-slides, hurricanes, and so on.

Violent blows. Cycles and processes to which people have assigned different names that have the same effects on people: joy or sorrow, gain or loss, pleasure or pain. Cycles that continued with a fierceness and determination that are merely life's expressions in all their complexities.

Totally enraptured in her stories, I'd forget what I was supposed to be doing until Ma's, "Hurry up an' finish what yuh doin', chile. Stop going backwards before life catch up an' run over yuh," jolted me back to the present.

Now, shaking off the lethargy of nostalgia of times before my time, I decided that I was ready to embrace Ma's spirit and join the line of women everywhere who'd said, "Enough was enough." I would drink of the Savannah River and then, like Scarlett O'Hara, shake my fist at the Georgian fiery night-sky and declare with unshakeable confidence that life was mine to define according to my terms. I, Indo-Trinidadian immigrant to the U.S., also possessed the will to get up and get on. No more days of gushing tears and screaming prayers that crashed into the heavens in thunderous bawls loud enough to awaken my Shepherdess from her slumber. No more expectation that my Shepherdess would answer with electrifying jolts to char my enemies into crisp blackness and shoot them instantaneously into Dante's Inferno.

I'd come to learn during sleepless midnight hours that my Shepherdess would have me realize my strength in the gentle whispers of Creator God who knew best that loud noise rips apart and destroys, and gentle sounds eased into my consciousness left indelible imprints upon my soul.

A while ago, I'd stopped raging and fuming and sometimes cursing, too, and heard for the first time God so quietly say, "Fret not yourself." And, "If I know where the sparrow falls, what makes you think I don't know everything about you? I know your every pain and joy—past, present, and future." Turbulent emotions calmed, I'd learned to recognize how God's peace could quietly start in my belly like a soft candle's glow, then tingle warmly down to my toes, then radiate effusively to the very crown of my head. Life affirming, touching, reassuring of my being, my womanhood, my very self.

One morning, I awoke as God's gentle massage bathed me afresh in a way that *no one* had ever touched me. I smiled at the rising sun with a newly birthed confidence and my spirit responded, "Yes!"

Until that rebirth, I still had to get a grip on things, experience many more ravages of life, wrestle against race, gender, age, and cultural discriminations in the pursuit of my dream in the land of dream-chasers.

*

My dream of being in law enforcement began shortly after I met Randolph Burroughs, the road leading to our meeting paved with convoluted twists and turns, loneliness and heartache.

I was the last of five children born to a forty-eight year-old mother and fifty-two year-old father, my father being my mother's second husband. Ma's first husband had died and left her with four children to raise alone, two boys and two girls. However, she did not remain a widow for long. When my father came along, Ma made clear that she was not tolerating any man with bed-hopping ways. Not that she didn't need him to help raise her four children who were grown and could take care of themselves. She just was not having any man come along at her age to disrespect her by simply wanting to shack up. Not she. She'd lived respectably with a man to whom she had been married before, and if another man wanted her then he had to marry her, too. Foot put down, my father married Ma and shortly thereafter I was born.

Then, Pa died when I was thirteen years young. He left no will because the making of a will was what only the rich and wealthy did. Everyone else depended on one's family doing the right thing, which was to offer as much assistance possible because blood's thicker than water. Supposedly. In our case, Pa's relatives treated us like we were his spit on a sunny, tropical day. Consequently, Ma, a housewife all her life, had to find a way to raise me without help or the promise of help from anyone. Her four older children by that time were married and raising their own families and couldn't be depended upon. All man jack was for himself. Nonetheless, with a clear vision for my future, Ma was determined that I received a good education.

To afford that, she turned to washing, starching, and ironing, decent but back-breaking service. Being a washerwoman was for the strong-backed whose initiation caused her to cry rivers of tears while she mastered the process to stand mistress of her domain. She first learned to catch the right amount of sunrays to make white cottons gleam bright. Next, she learned to boil the starch to the right consistency. No lumpiness: save that for cornmeal porridge. No thickness: thick starch was good only for hardening into a potential missile. In those days, many unwanted lovers didn't know what piece of dried starch zinged past him or found its target. No runniness: runny starch meant that the cotton wouldn't iron right. No matter how much she sprinkled and balled up the cotton shirt before ironing, if the starch had been too runny no amount of ironing made that shirt free of wrinkles.

Ironing was risky business, too, that demanded one's total focus. Heating that iron over a coal-pot that burned at the right temperature so that no soot escaped onto the iron and transferred onto the clothing was science in progress. Some women, who felt they were mistresses of the art, used ironing time to gossip. When the gossip became juicy—as we say in Trinidad—and concentration broke, and she forgot to test the iron with a lick of a finger then carelessly placed a too-hot iron on her best customer's best shirt, well, goodbye to that customer and hello to a smaller pay—or no pay.

I witnessed Ma become a mistress, her status ironically being perfected during the dry season, which brought more work than during the rainy season. I loved the dry season all the more for that reason but hated the rainy season, and not only because it brought rain-flies and mosquitoes. During the rainy season, worked dried up—also ironical—and on some days all we could do was cry buckets of tears, as if to tell the pregnant clouds that delivered their torrents they'd met their match in seeing who could produce more water. Cloudy or rainy days tested the most expert washer-woman. One, insufficient sunlight meant white shirts couldn't be spread out on the bleach—a mesh-wired bed—to be bleached whiter than lily. Two, the increased humidity that rain brought played havoc with starching and nothing could be done to get it right. And, three, well thankfully the only part of the process that wasn't affected was the ironing.

So, the rainy season lessened work and brought to the surface the merciless devils in some customers. They held steadfastly to their resolve of "no-work-no-pay" or "no-satisfaction-no-pay," a posture that indicted them of an attitude that bespoke a kind of boasting that their arms were long enough to box with nature—or God. They acted like the hill of their success couldn't one day be leveled, leaving them to bite into sour, forced-ripe mango or *pomme-cythere*.

But for the kindness of the affable ones who were blessed with a God-conscious regard for life and people, Ma and I would have lost all faith in humanity, especially me. Those dry and rainy seasons helped shape my own awareness of the two types of people I'd meet along life's path. Those who would always curse and blame people for the clouds and the rain, choosing to believe that people had some sort of electro-magnetic power to manipulate the weather to someone else's misfortune. Perpetual malcontents without compunction or guilt, they thought nothing of heaping indignities upon others. They would inflict wounds upon others then pour salt and pepper into them, stand back and watch and ask—sometimes as though mystified but more so in anger and impatience, "How come some people always sick and begging for mercy?" They'd then shrug their shoulders apathetically while repeating the question in a meaningless refrain in answer to pleas for a show of human compassion.

Then, there were others—few and far between—whose empathy flowed as thick and sweet as guava syrup, and my faith in God and humanity was restored. Ma, on the other hand, at age sixty-one, was only determined that I would never suffer the indignities of poverty, such as sucking on salt and chewing mint leaves to keep one's breath fresh-smelling so that nobody knew how hungry you really were. She was determined that the time would come when every night we went to bed with full bellies, slept contentedly, and awoke the next morning to enjoy a breakfast of bakes and sardines. She believed that sardines were the best brain food, and the brains of the last baby she brought into the world had to be best fortified to succeed in life. Without her having to say so, I knew that she expected me to make good of schooling at San

Juan Government School (the elementary school nearest our home) then at Osmond High School.

At age sixteen, I could no longer stand to see Ma struggling day in and day out to make ends meet. During my last term of high school, I found a part-time job in a restaurant, having convinced Ma that the afternoon and weekend hours wouldn't interfere with my chances to graduate. I persuaded her that all I had to do was wait tables, smile a lot to make good tips, and make sure the male customers kept their hands to themselves. Other Indian girls were doing it and had taught me how to put fast men in their place. If other girls could do it—and they weren't smarter than I was—then so could I. Ma couldn't bear the thought that I wasn't as smart as other girls and relented. I think she was also secretly proud of me. After all, in elementary school I was never held back or demoted because subsequent teachers wrote in my report card that I loved to daydream, was then admitted into Osmond without any problems, and then set to graduate with my class. I also added that with my little income she wouldn't have to scrub her fingers raw on the jooking-board (scrubbing board).

My training period on the job wasn't even over when my I met a young man, twenty-four years old, who swept me off my feet, literally. He was a handsome *dougla* (half East Indian-half African). Always very well dressed and seeming always to have money in his pocket, with his excessively generous tips he impressed me all the more in the face of Ma's lifelong struggle and hardship. He was also a fast talker, with a tongue that could have charmed a sparrow from her nest, and a with swagger that said, "Step aside! Get outta my way!" His conversations boasted that Trinidad was his for the taking and I was naïve enough to believe him. After all, he was the first young man like that I'd met. Sauvé. Sophisticated. Worldly-wise. Confident.

By the time I'd graduated he'd begun visiting me at home and every time brought a gift for both me and Ma. In fact, he spent money on us like stupid, as we say back home. Generosity in pants, it was as though he was sent straight from heaven, so I ignored that niggling feeling that a price tag was attached. Besides, I was too happy for Ma's momentary relief from financial uncertainty and half-heartedly agreed with her that he was such a good, sweet, generous, thoughtful young man who loved me. It wasn't long before he made clear that he expected something in return. Half-heartedly believing myself to be in love, but more so in gratitude, I eventually surrendered to his sweet nothingness, my virginity exchanged for an unplanned, untimely pregnancy, which I kept secret until I began to show.

Ma recovered from the shock that I wasn't just getting fat on the day she bumped into my belly—deliberately so, I know now—and felt the firmness of life and not the jiggle of a Jell-O bowl. She didn't even give me a speech, like I expected. Instead, she got straight down to brass tacks and asked me when we planned to get married, as if my young man and I were making such plans and keeping them from her.

"Yuh gettin' marrid tomorrow, or what," she said in her quiet Ma-way.

"I ent kno' wha' yuh talkin' about, Ma. Who say I planning to get marrid? And where all dis talk 'bout marriage comin' from?" I hemmed and hawed, as shame began to blanket me and rushed to answer my own question with the hope that a red herring would work, "I, I doh know what yuh mean, Ma. What yuh talkin' about? Marrid? That's the last thing on my mind. Besides, I much too young for that." I could feel my insides churning nervously. I was really too young to even think of getting married. Not me.

She continued quietly, using Creole so I knew she meant business and that was no time for *stupidness* (absurdity). She slipped into Creole on those rare occasions as she did then, "Doh try to make *sut*[1] of me, chile, or *mamaguy* (tomfool) me because all sunlight show de same crack in de same vase. I only want to know w'en de baby due, and yuh better say that I have enough time to plan a decent wedding. You ent going to be the cause of my shame. Till the day I die, I want to sway muh hips wid muh head held high when I walk in de village."

I couldn't bring myself to look her in the face. Her obvious disappointment and deep hurt were enough to drive me to my knees and mumble my sorries, tears streaming unchecked down my cheeks. She just patted my bowed head and retreated to her room.

I rose to my feet a few minutes later, took my sniffles to my room, and crept into bed with a dull feeling and full awareness that Ma's word was final. Because she upheld the strictest standards of propriety, I knew that I was to marry the jackanapes of whom I knew little to

---

1   Meaning, fool.

nothing about—except that he gave liberally—so that the baby would be born in wedlock.

The wedding was as dull as the day was gray, its specifics quickly receding to that place in my mind from which I purposely recalled nothing. I married him because it was expected of me and I continued to give myself to him because it was my duty—and because I was grateful for his easing our hardship. Still, that virgin part of me remained detached from my submissiveness and gratitude.

Lynn was born shortly after my seventeenth birthday, then, one year later on my eighteenth birthday Anthony was born, and the extent of my husband's nothingness became evident. Anthony's birth, with a congenital heart murmur and mental problems, relayed the dispassionate nature of his conception. Poor little thing, I often thought, as I sometimes gazed at him when I had the courage to do so. I didn't dare love him too much, this helpless extension of myself who too often at night struggled to breathe and stay alive. Yet, I dared to love him too much despite his blank stare that interrupted his obvious awareness of his environment, one that he filled with gentleness and much kindness. He taught me that he dared to live and love. Later in life, those memories of his daring energized me, too. Life was meant for the living.

While the children were too young to be aware of anything much, I was beyond dismay—more so for Ma than for myself because Ma thought that the sun rose and set on her son-in-law's head—to learn that their father was a mere conman and headed for jail because of a failed scheme in which he was caught. Thus began a recidivist pattern of his being released from jail, becoming involved in another con, failing, getting caught, and returning to jail. Through it all, I was to stand by my man. So, I stood.

I decided to attend one of his court cases in Tunapuna to show some moral support. After all, he was still my husband, despite the fact that he was emerging as just another good-for-nothing Trinidadian scamp, a description Ma simply refused to accept.

During the hearing, I sat next to a young fellow East Indian woman named Sheila with whom I hit it off. Fortuitously, Sheila was the girlfriend of Randolph Burroughs, then an ambitious young policeman, and she introduced us to each other. During the introduction, I was quite aware that I had a similar effect on him as I had on other men. I was still young, extremely pretty and turning men's heads wherever I went. My figure showed no tell-tale signs that I'd given birth to two children, and when it suited me I kept that information to myself. My business was mine.

Later, I reflected upon how Sheila was secure enough of her relationship with Randolph and not at all threatened by his open admiration of me. Sheila's security, however, lay in the fact that even though she was the mother of a son who was not even his, she *and* her son were already living with him and his mother, and wedding plans were in the making. It later became publically known that his mother loved and accepted only an East Indian woman for her son's wife. Sheila and my friendship grew rapidly over the following months, and I was her maid-of-honor at their small, private wedding ceremony.

Our friendship enveloped Randolph who, in no uncertain terms, made it clear the type of man to whom I was married. He had no patience for men who may have started off on the wrong side of the law but made no effort to turn their lives around. He'd seen that my husband at the court house and noted that he was totally lacking in ambition, one of those who was contented to remain on that dead-end track. Randolph, on the other hand, was determined to leave behind a notable reputation. He freely shared how he and a few of his friends had turned their lives around. They were boys who'd become men, having put aside their boyhood fancies of playing cops and robbers and cowboys and Indians for the reality of respectable careers. He was determined, through hard work and sheer force of will and ambition, to make a name for himself in law enforcement.

He, like his mother, preferred East Indian women because they totally supported their men, not seemingly in competition with them. He frequently claimed that only women like Sheila and I apparently understood that men's driving force, in his case to rise in the ranks and earn his promotion to Inspector, was a good thing for society. Consequently, he believed I was married to the wrong man and offered to assist me when I was ready to divorce him, because divorce him the vagabond I must. He convinced me that I could do much better for myself.

As our friendship continued to grow, he introduced me to many people in law enforcement who impressed me. I decided that I wanted to pursue a similar career. I was at this time attending Johnson Commercial School in San Juan and learning secretarial skills. It was something I was doing because career opportunities for Indian women were limited like they were those for any Trinidadian woman who had to work for a living. We were limited to becoming secretaries, nurses, government clerks, or teachers. But I'd wanted more for myself, as well as to be in the position to help young people turn away from crime toward getting a good education so they could have a better life for themselves.

Then, Trinidad opened the doors of laws enforcement to women; however, the standards under British colonial rule for becoming a police officer were very strict. A woman must be five feet, six inches tall. I was only five feet, four inches. Such ambition thwarted, I settled on being a secretary at Martin Looby Contracting Company in Marine Square and moved to St. James, a suburb a few miles west of the Port of Spain, to be conveniently closer to my job.

Lynn and Anthony remained with Ma.

I was only twenty years old when life in the country's capital offered its social fruits for my picking.

Chapter 2 — A Tributary of Life

While living in St. James, I met the famous captain of Invaders Steel Band, Elliot "Ellie" Mannette.[2] At work, he was all the other secretaries talked about during the Carnival season. From Monday through Friday they talked constantly about the previous Saturday-night fete: which panman (a steelband player or pan builder) went home with what girl. Or, they speculated on the coming fete and who would leave with whom. They all angled to go home with him, despite his marital status. Out of curiosity, I decided one Saturday night to go with them and see who this man was, whether he was worth the gossip. From that first time, I was in love. After catching his eye across the dance floor, I boldly approached him, asked him to dance, and during that dance I knew my fate was sealed and determined to be the one to leave with him. To be with him forever.

Ours was a passionate affair, full of all the thrills and dangers that were characteristic of an extramarital one. At first, I kept up my deception well; I maintained well the persona of a young woman who'd never been married or had any maternal obligations: my secret.

My post-natal stomach was as flat as it was at age thirteen, which

---

2   See the full story in Nurse's *Unheard Voices*.

drew a combination of admiration and jealousy from Iris, the half-sister who was closest to me. Helping me get dressed for Anthony's name-giving ceremony, she exclaimed, "Buh look at yuh belly, nuh! Is like yuh never had a baby, much less two! Or maybe it's because you have dark skin, like your father. Sometimes, I wish my father was dark-skinned, too, so I could have nice, dark skin like yours. I so detest this light skin we got from our father. Some people lucky, too bad."

I'd later wished she'd said "lucky, for so" instead of "lucky, too bad." People used "for so" to signal amazement or wonder and "too bad" to mean "you slept in the bed of your own making." So, too bad I couldn't have a name-giving celebration for Lynn because Ma didn't want people counting from the time I got married to the time she was born and start snickering at us. Too bad that Anthony's birth was without any shadow of shame yet he was mentally impaired. Innocent of sin but guilty for having been born into this world so full of sin. Living in St. James, none of this threatened my façade. I was young, beautiful, with a body that guarded my two precious secrets, and simply determined to enjoy my youth while I still could.

So, I competed for and won the distinction of being Ellie's main (woman), and with wanton disregard that he was married I told all of Port of Spain that his wife wore his wedding ring but I owned his heart. We frequently met at Franco House, the rendezvous beach house in Carenage for lovers; I was his party-girl at all the parties; and once at a party when his wife confronted me and demanded that I lay off her husband, I had the gall to fight her and then use the fight to my benefit.

During the following years, I continued to ignore her grief for which I was partly responsible, but when she died a few years later I felt conflicted. The doctors said she died of a broken heart because there was nothing wrong with her. She just gave up on life. It was like she willed death and death eventually claimed its legacy. Her untimely death shook me deeply, so when the opportunity arose for me to immigrate to the U.S. in 1962, I seized it. It was high time to end my affair with a married man; besides, an affair with a married man was full of too many disappointments, the major one being that husbands seldom, if ever, left their wives. All this I'd learn later in life. At the time, I'd been too full of youthful apathy to anyone's feelings but mine.

I viewed my decision to make a clean cut of things as a good one. I further decided to cut off not only Ellie but all other friends. The only one I'd remain in touch with was Ma and would forge new friends in the States. All this time, I failed to recognize that I sometimes had a tendency to go to the extremes.

Lynn and Anthony, thirteen and twelve years young, continued in Ma's care when I left Trinidad, still full of hope that life was mine for taking. Intuitively, however, I knew that I would never see my loving Anthony again. Shortly after immigrating, Ma wrote to say that he had become too much for her to handle and wanted permission to institutionalize him. I granted her permission. Two years later, she wrote that he'd passed away.

I grieved the loss of a son with whom I'd dared not bond too tightly. Didn't I know that his stay was like a fragile gift, a fleeting whisper, a glistening tear that tugged at the heart of those who dared to love and appreciate him? A year later, Ma followed him. I dreamt of him, a healthy young man, standing on the banks of a river whose water was crystal clear, greeting Ma with a smile and a hug. That dream warmed my heart and comforted me at my double loss of two precious souls. Ma was seventy-eight years old. With no one to take care of Lynn, I sent for her.

*

At the time, I was living in Flushing, Queens and working as a receptionist at Blumenthal & Company in Manhattan, New York. I remained there for three years then grew tired of working for a button-manufacturing company that offered no chances for improving my lot and applied for a job at the Post Office in Flushing. My being hired was a god-sent answer to my dream of social mobility. The serendipity to it was its location; I could walk to work! No more commuting!

My starting salary at the post office was two dollars and twenty-five cents per hour. Later, the workers unionized to ameliorate our salary and raises, which encouraged me to remain there for fifteen years working as a clerk. Sorting First Class Mail was not intellectually demanding or challenging. One needed only remain alert to do one's work well.

I would have remained living in Flushing for the rest of my life but that New York weather began to take its toll on me. I could never reconcile how the warmth of sunshine brought no relief during the bitingly cold winter months, especially to my fingertips. After a mere fifteen minutes in the outdoors, my fingers and thumbs were so achingly cold, I'd bite my lips to stop crying in pain. My toes ached, too. When I complained, no one else seemed to have my problem, which made me feel like I was a Martian from outer space who couldn't survive on this planet. Much later, when I was being treated for hypothyroidism, I learned that the body's extremities reacted this way to cold weather and had little to nothing to do with where I was born.

Certainly, I missed the land of my birth where sunshine meant delicious warmth commingled with the brilliant array of a variety of petunias, lilies, chrysanthemums, chrysanthemums, hibiscuses, crocuses, orchids and their tantalizing fragrances. Snow, on the other hand, had no appeal to me. It fell, and its whiteness quickly yielded to gray and brown and a slippery mess upon which I had to dance like an ill-trained figure skater to avoid falling onto. Every winter brought a deep yearning for the sight of my dazzling Caribbean colors—and Carnival. How I sometimes missed Carnival and its energy!

After fifteen years of wintry blasts, each subsequent one as shocking as the first, I decided to find a more weather-friendly place to live. I had a very dear friend, Grace Smith, who lived in Atlanta, Georgia. Our friendship had begun in Trinidad and continued like a river whose two tributaries were separated by some obstacles then to be rejoined. We'd reconnected in New York just before she migrated to Atlanta. Ours was a dear, warm friendship—despite Grace being five years my junior—that led to my becoming the godmother of her gorgeous daughter, Arlene. Grace can be described as a vivacious Trinidadian Creole, meaning she was of mixed ancestry, but in the U.S. identified as black. Her insistent invitation to Atlanta was a clarion call to our reunion, a call I was finding harder to resist. One cold wintry day, to escape New York's frigid weather, I headed south for some warmth. I immediately fell in love with the climate. True, it was a little cold but by no means did it afflict a bone-chilling coldness that ached tearfully my poor fingers and thumbs. I also loved the less hectic pace and southern hospitality, so my decision to relocate to Georgia in 1980 was easy.

I put in for and was granted a transfer, after a delay that seemed interminable, to the Atlanta Post Office. I didn't mind that I didn't get the same position I had in Queens and accepted the position of a mail handler, with the expectation that when a clerical one became available I would apply. The mail handler position required the lifting of heavy boxes, packages, cases, and so on. Much to my consternation, after only three months I hurt my back while pushing a heavy cart called a gurney. I was sent to the medical unit, whose doctor recommended that I remain off my feet for one month. After I returned to work, I continued to be on medication to alleviate the pain which seemed to intensify due to the nature of my work.

In the face of unrelenting pain, I made the reluctant decision to resign and fortunately got another job as a security officer at the Atlanta Airport, now called Hartsfield Jackson Airport. I was assigned to Delta Airlines' baggage claim where I checked the passengers' baggage to verify that baggage tickets matched the claims. A routine position that demanded neither physical nor mental exertion, it was made somewhat interesting by observing who claimed what or who carried what. Teens and hikers with backpacks, backpacks becoming fashionable also for college students in sweat shirts with their school's names emblazoned on them in pride. Business people with garment bags and briefcases, all briskly going about their business. Women struggling with cosmetic pieces whose contents were the only reason the struggle was worthwhile, I often mused. An almost mind-numbing position, I then became bored with identifying people by luggage and wondered how much longer I could take it. Even less enticing was its minimum wage salary, a reduction from the Post Office's salary, and one I couldn't afford because I needed more than minimum wage to provide for myself and Lynn, who was not yet living on her own.

*

Lynn was the closest living person to my heart. She was all I had left in this world, my half-siblings and their children not being as close as I would have liked. We'd all made choices based upon what was best for us, and I refused to apologize for or regret any of mine. Instead, I'd be thankful for what life had given me so far, including my generous, warm-hearted daughter whose medical condition should not be a cause for shame for her. She'd been diagnosed with bi-polar, and as long as she remained on her meds she was a delight and joy. However, when she stopped taking her meds, she was a delightful pain that I'd want to hug or slap and say, "Stop being so stupid, especially with your kindness to others,"

With a heart toward helping others, she often over-extended herself first then second-guessed herself afterward. She constantly pulled along me and her own daughter Kim in the wake of her heartbreaks and disappointments. Life with Lynn was a roller-coaster of thrills followed by despair. I had no problems navigating both ends of the spectrum with Lynn and had passed on my own brand of wisdom to my granddaughter, Kim.

At the moment, Lynn was home living with me, so I often overheard her end of the phone conversations with Kim. Kim, who was as pragmatic as I, gave Lynn advice to which Lynn always protested that she was the mother and Kim the daughter, and that she didn't have to listen to Kim. I paused long enough to listen and figure out what Kim most likely said, then resumed my business. I was reassured that Lynn would be all right, sandwiched between me and Kim, two women whose feet were planted firmly on the ground.

During my daily quiet time, I pondered that the joy-sorrow-joy of female blood relationships must have begun somewhere, sometime with Mother-Daughter. After all, Jesus must have had a Sister born of Their Shared Mother. Yet, this Mother and Daughter have remained nameless not because they don't exist but because they're strong and powerful enough to sacrifice their Voices for Father and Son. Then, in the fullness of time, Mother's Voice will sound out again, and men once more will submit peacefully to Mother's Supreme will. Until then, humans will continue to sacrifice in necessary-needless acts of aggression their handsome sons and beautiful daughters, the latest one in the land where language confusion began, ancient Babylon now called Iraq.

How I continue to pray daily for Lynn's son Jimmy, my grandson, who served there. My heart equally burst with pride and pain for him and all other grand-babies fighting for peace. Jimmy is just as precious to me as all soldiers are to their families. It makes no difference that he, a strapping member of the U.S. Air Force, is handsome enough to head to Hollywood and double for The Rock. He resembles The Rock so much that people often approach him and ask for his autograph. As one who fully supports the soldiers, I pray daily not only for Jimmy and his battalion but for all those involved, American or Iraqi. I grieve with all those who lose a loved one fighting to preserve the American Dream, and I mourn the loss of all those precious lives, American, Iraqi, British, Italian, Japanese, Australian, and the entire host of the deceased of the Coalition of the Willing, and the unwilling, too.

How I champion those Americans who still bear courageously the ideals of freedom and democracy for all men, women, and children. But wasn't peace the higher ideal? People have enough to contend with when nature unleashes her fury and wipes out hundreds and thousands in one fell swoop, whether to an earthquake, hurricane, tsunami, volcano, or other natural disaster. Sichuan. Nargis. Katrina. Janet. Indonesia. Montserrat. Kick Em Jenny. Pompeii. Where and when does the list begin? When will it end?

LIFE. Living in fervent expectation. And backwards. Expressing fervidly incessant longings.

I love life and refuse to spend much time harboring regrets. With my fierce spirit to win, I've said to every form of adversity and foe, "Bring it on." Never one to run from a fight, still nothing in life in Trinidad or New York prepared me for what came with being a sergeant deputy sheriff at the Atlanta's Fulton County Sheriff Department.

*

Realizing that I'd go crazy should I remain at the job in Baggage Claim, I began to explore other options. Upon inquiring from co-workers at the airport, I learned that some better-paying jobs required one to carry a weapon; however, such required certification. Further inquiry informed me that a course was being given for all law enforcement personnel who wanted to be certified. The course required the completion of an oral and a written exam, as well as going to a gun range. At my age, in my middle fifties in 1984, I decided to rise to the challenge and enrolled in the course.

The course, offered at Atlanta University, was being taught by Captain Richard B. Lankford of the Fulton County Sheriff Department.

Lankford was a dynamic, handsome, African American young man of thirty-four years. Since 1979, he served as the pastor of Springfield Baptist Church in Hogansville, a task he took as seriously as he did his work in law enforcement. He was not only the church's pastor but also its organist and choir director. His religious duties demanded his preparing sermons, bible studies, chairing church committees, and holding choir rehearsals. These pastoral and law enforcement demands he balanced with his family obligations, having been married for ten years and helping his wife raise their seven-year-old son and six-year-old daughter.

While teaching the course, he informed the class that he was running for sheriff. The media were replete with news of this very important race. The present sheriff had been in office for sixteen years and his son was preparing to replace him. Reportedly also, the jail had very few female deputies because the women (who weren't required to meet the standards of the deputies) were being called matrons, and segregation still existed among the workers. Cpt. Lankford announced that his decision to run was motivated by a strong desire to bring change to an institution that was still defined by white male privilege. He solicited and was promised the support of every member of the class.

The following year, 1985, Cpt. Lankford won easily, having established his reputation in the community as a sound leader of high religious and moral principles. It was with additional pride that he earned the distinction of being the first black to be elected sheriff in the history of Georgia, but not without some controversy. For instance, his opponent ran an ad that darkened Lankford's light skin—he was biracial, born to a white mother and black father—which did not dampen his chances since he defeated his opponent by sixteen thousand votes. Many of those votes came from whites who crossed over to give him the largest percentage of white votes in Fulton County's history.

For the part I played in voting for him, I was very proud. I'd grown to admire considerably a man who juggled his many responsibilities yet found time to mentor others. I found him to be remarkable and myself to be lucky to be inspired by a young, talented, brilliant pillar of our community. The entire class similarly shared my enthusiasm and I went one step further, at his suggestion, to apply for a deputy position in July 1985, at Fulton County Sheriff Department. I was ecstatic to be hired the very next month and work with my teacher, motivator, and mentor. Finally, I could stop feeling like I was picking around the edges of the world.[3]

I was so excited that I immediately wrote to Randolph and Sheila, with whom I'd maintained contact, to share my good news. Shortly thereafter, in response I received their warmest congratulations, best wishes, and a photograph of Randolph in uniform when he was promoted to commissioner. Commissioner?! The news surprised and pleased me but reminded that I'd not kept in touch with them as I should have. He'd sailed past the ranks to the top and I was only vaguely aware of his meteoric rise. I vowed to pay closer attention to Trinidad news and learned of his Flying Squad that maintained law and order in the country. I was delighted that he'd done well for himself and being a positive influence to society.

Randolph's photo filled me with a wave of nostalgia for home and I was momentarily back in Trinidad visiting the beach in Point Cumana, climbing over the limbs of fallen palm trees, picking up and examining almonds to find an edible one that was so delicious when mingled with the salty sea water, smelling the salty sea breeze that mingled with the aroma of fried fish and curried meats unique to Point Cumana village. The memories of home coupled with the prospects of serving in my new job gave me a heady feeling of life's goodness. It was terrific to be alive!

Grace also returned my phone call, excited that things were going my way. "And, to think yuh wasted precious time in New York when yuh could've been in Atlanta all along and doing what yuh always wanted to do."

"I know, chile," I responded. "But you and I know that nutten happen before its time."

"I still waitin'," she said.

"Waitin' fuh what?"

"To hear yuh say that I was right in getting yuh down here. That's what."

I laughed, "A'right then. You was right."

"An'?"

"An' you told me so. Satisfied now?"

---

3   See Toni Morrison's *Song of Solomon*, p. 235.

"But of course," she laughed, "and next time, you wouldn't be so hard-head to listen to good advice."

We continued to chat about her day and she brought me up-to-date with news on Arlene, my god-daughter, whom I'd neglected. We ended the call with my promise to visit them on that Sunday for dinner.

I went to bed that night feeling that life was good to me.

*

My letter of appointment informed me to report to the jail, to the area where most of the newly hired deputies began.

For the first time in a long while, I began to feel I could breathe. I would earn a sizeable, reliable income that would allow me to save toward the purchase of my own house. No more renting and putting my money into a pocket with holes. I finally began to feel that the U.S. was home, not merely the land of immigrants to which I had no loyalties.

Upon completion of the orientation, which provided my job description, I was quite surprised when the chief jailer, Chief Brownlee, offered me the choice of shift from among the three: 7 - 3, the day shift; 3 - 11, the afternoon shift; and 11 - 7, the night shift. Brownlee, white, was respected for the fair way he dealt with the few female deputies. I opted for the afternoon one and was further surprised when he answered in the affirmative but that I would have to have my days off during the week until I'd earned some seniority. Once I had seniority, I could put in a bid for weekends off. Until then, I was assigned Mondays and Tuesdays off, for many years.

I began working in what was called the old jail, a new jail set to be completed in the near future. The old jail had those big keys, which probably gave rise to the term "turnkey," because the doors to those keys were extremely heavy, some of them very hard to close. My first job was simple: I clocked in, took roll call of all the inmates on my floor, saw that they received their meals, took them to sick call, and escorted them to church on Wednesday nights and Sundays. They were strictly forbidden from divulging the whats and whys of their incarceration. That was for the judges and lawyers to address. Deputy sheriffs were responsible for keeping them safe until they were transferred to prison.

The jail was merely a holding place until their respective cases were settled. Managing the incarcerated was the easiest part of my job for that part posed no distractions. Thus far, I was able to apply myself diligently and conscientiously to my work, and in December I proudly received my Certificate of Completion of required work in "Policy and Procedures."

My first accident gave me a glimpse into the way the bureaucratic wheel of the department turned. While serving the inmates dinner one evening in April, 1986, I twisted my right wrist when opening the cell door, as the handle was very difficult to turn. I made a note of the incident in my notebook but did not file an accident report, thinking nothing of the injury. However, two days later when my wrist began to swell and hurt even worse than winter-cold fingers, I knew it was more serious and reported it to the two captains. They advised me that there was nothing they could do because of the forty-eight-hour lapse, but that I should report the accident to the watch commander and seek medical attention. Heeding their advice, I visited my private physician who ordered an X-ray, the results of which showed a bad sprain. My doctor prescribed four to six months of therapy. However, I couldn't be reimbursed for my own out-of-pocket expenses because I didn't follow through with the reporting of the accident on time.

Looking back now, I think that incident taught me *always* to follow Policy and Procedure and *never* to take anything for granted.

In 1987, I took the sergeant's test and passed, and also completed the "Officer Survival" seminar and the Jail Officer Certification.

In July 1988, because I was recognized as a powerhouse, I was promoted to Sergeant Deputy Sheriff and completed the required supervisory training. I also became a professional member of the American Jail Association.

Sheriff Lankford, also having risen through the ranks, knew every aspect of his job. No ifs, ands, or buts about that fact. He'd won the election because of what he knew and brought to the job; he maintained his position and title for the same reasons. Nonetheless, his election had not gone over well with his enemies, some of who were determined to see the first elected black man fall.

His chief at the jail was another officer who knew his job very well, too: Chief Brownlee, previously mentioned. Like the other deputies, I came to respect him for his decency, fairness, and professionalism.

*

Once more, immersed in building my career I lost track of Randolph and Sheila and was pulled up short by a friend who'd returned with the news of Randolph's arrest for murder. I had him repeat the news to make sure that I'd heard right. Murder?! He confirmed that I'd heard correctly and continued that Trinidadians liked to keep people in their place, too bad. Apparently, some people didn't like the amount of power that his Flying Squad wielded and somebody brought up murder charges against him. I was beyond indignant. After all the good he'd done for the country and keeping the place relatively free from criminals who wanted to take over and run the show, somebody was trying to destroy him and his family.

I contemplated writing Sheila and showing moral support. But when I sat down to write, nothing I wrote sounded right. I just couldn't find the appropriate words. Surrendering to sending her positive energy and thoughts across the Atlantic Ocean, I wished her health and strength and followed the printed news. I was tremendously relieved to read when all charges were dropped but desolate when shortly thereafter he resigned his commission. We people, our own people did that to him and broke his heart. He died a few months later. Sheila, who couldn't live without her one true love and best friend, died the following year. I was grief-stricken and blamed myself for getting all this news second-hand or from the newspapers. I tried to ease my conscience that it was life in America that was to be blamed. Scrambling to make a living, becoming too busy for busyness sake, too busy for our own damn good, for what?

Life in the States meant none of dropping in on a friend or family member without an invitation or a phone call to announce one's arrival. None of Saturdays and Sundays of people coming by casually and staying for ole talk and drinks. And such was expected. People who didn't socialize in this way missed out on being informed on the gossip on the village or town. No Christmas *parang*[4] in exchange for rum punch and black cake, which made the Christmas season just as unique as the Carnival season, and for some Trinidadians who rolled both seasons into one, those months served as one long extended holiday. I sometimes missed that laissez-faire approach to everything.

Keeping track of the news of my friend's vilification and its subsequent fatal effects shook me. Randolph was the image of life and strength with a big heart that he'd extended to his country. He was its protector and provider of order and stability. He occupied in a corner of my mind the indomitable image of the father, husband, and son of which I couldn't boast. Yet, life had broken his spirit and will to live, and Sheila's, too.

For the next few days, I mourned them in memory and spirit.

Recently, I read as crime rates in Trinidad and Tobago soared to ridiculous proportions that people yearned for another Randolph Burroughs to arrive. They longed for the return of the days of his rigorous, disciplined squad that kept criminals and would-be criminals in check. Those were years, they lamented, when people went about their business without fear of being mugged, kidnapped, or killed. They wanted back being able to retire for the night without fear of being awaken in terror at the sound of their doors being broken down, husbands being slashed with machetes and left to bleed out while their wives were raped and brutalized, and afterwards their homes being emptied of appliances that could be peddled. Shortly thereafter, I read of the Flying Squad being resurrected and the country cheering their welcome. To which I added, "Smile in your grave, dear friend, for you did well. You still do, and I hope it's not too late for the return of people's peace of mind."

---

4   See Allsop's *Dictionary of Caribbean English Usage*: "practice of house-to-house serenading by groups singing religious songs in Trinidad Spanish Creole, especially at Christmas, accompanied by cuatros and other musical instruments.

CHAPTER 3 — FLOWING AROUND THE OBSTACLES

In 1989, I realized that in order to protect not only my job but the job of all deputies and officers at the Fulton County Sheriff Department, we'd have to unionize. I approached two African American deputies, Sergeants Harmon and Walker who were organizing to this end to inquire about their progress. Learning that they were not having much luck, I agreed to join them. My job in New York taught me that membership in a union was necessary. Being at the mercy of employers who cared not one iota about employees was too risky.

Immediately, my urgency and determination became so contagious that the two men allowed me to take the reins, agreeing to assist me in any possible way. I was more than honored at their confidence in my leadership that led me to becoming a co-president of the union. They respected my age and the little wisdom I offered. Together, the three of us plotted our course of action.

First, we visited Chip Warren and Dennis Hammock of the International Brotherhood of Police Officers (IBPO) Union to arrange a meeting with Sheriff Lankford. We needed his approval to canvass all the deputies to join. Lankford was fully supportive of our efforts and wrote a letter to Chief Brownlee at the jail expressing this. Next, we made appointments to meet with the six commissioners. One of them, Commissioner Roach, was the first to support the effort. He was a former pilot with Delta and knew the benefits of being unionized. He greeted us amicably and maintained cordiality with us. Only one of the commissioners was against the call to unionize and said so. He offered to present his arguments at the first meeting at the Assembly Hall, and reluctantly we agreed. After all, everyone had the right to speak. Wasn't that the democratic way?

Becoming organized had all the setbacks of a toddler mastering the stairs. At the first meeting in March, the other co-president and the treasurer of the executive board were no-shows. At the following, the secretary wasn't there, so Deputy Marlena Johnson agreed upon my request to record the minutes. Marlena, an African American, and I'd become friends after she was assigned to work with me. I'd soon noticed that we were compatible for many reasons. She and I shared similar work ethics—work hard, be helpful to others to the best of one's ability, and be positive. She was married with one son, and though she was positive and often a ray of sunlight, hers was a no-nonsense attitude that kept the male deputies in their social place around her. Her "don't-mess-with-me" manner was interpreted as "stuck-up," which didn't faze her in the least. I admired her for how well she did her job and commanded everyone's respect.

At this March meeting, I was so frustrated and angry that all I could do was fume in my seat about how blasted idiotic people were. When I became as angry as I was, the stringent Christian line, which according to St. Paul separated the old woman from the new, was erased and some salty language resurfaced unchecked, as it did at that moment. What the bloody hell good was the power of a co-president if unable to persuade others, including the executives, to attend a meeting that protected everyone's interest? Why the dickens was I elected in the first blasted place? All because one person nominated me and no one else had the guts to challenge the bloody nomination? And, what the blooming hell was wrong with these damn people?

Was my position merely symbolic of those who walked backwards and had no voice, like damn *douens*, as we said back home in Trinidad? Douens were folkloric people whose feet were turned backwards, which meant that though moving forward they were going nowhere.

According to Trinidadian artist LeRoy Clarke, their bellies were filled with gravel so when they opened their mouths to speak not words but howls of pain—or nothingness—emitted. Here in Atlanta, Georgia, it seemed like our attempts to unionize were being navigated by douens. "Not me, Maria," I fumed, "I ain't no damn douen! I will show them!" There and then, I determined that I would persist toward our goal, and the meeting ended with this resolve firmly planted in my mind as the mouth of the river to which I would flow.

The April meeting was a public one and a sheer disaster. First to speak was the lawyer who represented the Union, the IBPO. He was followed by Sergeant Harmon. They presented a strong, persuasive case for our unionizing. But the one who really took the cake, as the saying goes in Trinidad, was Captain Caudell Jones, an African American I thought we could count on. But what a Janus! When it was time for him to address the gathering, he said that he didn't think it was a good idea for the deputies to unionize at this time. His backtracking gave the commissioner, the one who didn't support the effort from the beginning, the chance to turn things around completely. He instructed the county lawyer to check the by-laws for a second time to see what was said regarding a resolution. Then he turned to the secretary and asked her to check the previous month's meeting for what was recorded because he was pretty sure someone was told to check the by-laws. The secretary said she couldn't find any such directive in the minutes. Obviously, Marlena, who'd served as ad hoc recorder of the last meeting, failed to make that note, if indeed the commissioner had made that request. Now, he was determined to make her look like a fool. That asshole! I fumed, completely flabbergasted. He and Jones both had that smug look on their faces. As for Jones, his wasn't even of a crabs-in-a-barrel mentality because he was out of the barrel and determined to keep everyone else inside.

Stewing in my anger, I couldn't even come to Marlena's defense because I'd angrily blanked out the end of the meeting. Now, I could feel my blood pressure rising. Poor recording or someone's poor memory, vague by-laws, and what seemed to be sheer delay tactics were about to ensure that we never even made it to the first step much less the top of the stairs! What a joke!

The next meeting in May was unforgettable. It was called to order at nine o'clock that morning. The negative commissioner was the first to speak after the minutes was read. He was brusque and wasted no time in getting straight to the point. First, he was against dues deduction. Then, he was afraid if the County allowed a new union, all these unions would bring the County to its knees. At that point, after only thirty minutes and while he was still speaking, all of the deputies, following my lead, quietly rose and left. It was a silent statement of our disagreement, initiated spontaneously and unanimously spoken that we would not be browbeaten.

The next day, I learned that the meeting was rescheduled for the following month. That June meeting was another exercise in futility and ended with everything being tabled for the July meeting, which also proved futile for it produced nothing because IBPO was not even on the agenda. However, lo and behold, the secretary was there! Hip, hip, hooray! I booed flatly. I didn't care that I was being sarcastic when I should have been positive. The time for my showing a semblance of diplomacy had come and gone.

Still determined not to surrender, we three—Harmon, Walker, and I—organized so many subsequent meetings the following months due to delays and postponements that it wasn't long before we earned the moniker of "The Three Musketeers." Due to our unrelenting persistence, finally everyone came to a consensus and we were granted a charter, which was called IBPO Local 453 and I was elected a co-president.

The Three Musketeers had the satisfaction of proving wrong all the nay-sayers who said it couldn't be done.

Ever mindful that I'd earned my dream job at an age when some people were looking to retire, I completed the necessary paperwork to participate in Fulton County's pension plan, as well as took and passed the required medical tests that ensured that I was not a health-risk to the job. Relieved that the uncertainty of pension was no longer an issue, I could focus on others matters such as the politics of the jail.

*

Meanwhile, much to my dismay, Sheriff Lankford was indicted on several charges, one of which was tax evasion. I, along with several deputies, made certain of being at the hearings. Seated next to me during one hearing was a New York reporter. We both observed how the sitting judge, who was white, paid scant attention to the evidence being presented. At one point, he actually fell asleep. Another time, he brusquely ordered the witnesses to hurry up with their statements because he had to go home and feed his wife's cat. The reporter and I couldn't believe our eyes and ears. I myself was convinced that Lankford's lawyer would be sure to ask for the judge to be removed but he never did. At yet another time, the judge refused to allow the jurors to hear certain witnesses who spoke on behalf of Lankford. He, however, allowed the IRS people to testify, and their testimony cleared Lankford of the tax evasion charges. All the other charges were so clearly fabricated and weak that both the New York reporter and I were convinced that he would be cleared of all charges. In fact, everyone else was similarly convinced, including one TV Channel 5 reporter who left saying that he was going to cover another court case.

Thus, when the verdict was announced that Lankford was guilty, pandemonium broke out in the court house. All we deputies were so infuriated we couldn't contain our anger. We so loudly protested at the clear miscarriage of justice that we had to be put out. Never had we witnessed an innocent man being so railroaded. Our loud protests continued outside the court house and erupted into violence. One deputy got into a brief altercation with a cameraman who decided to file charges against the deputy. He claimed that the deputy hit him first. Since I was present and witnessed everything firsthand, I was subpoenaed to testify. With a clear conscience and without hesitation, I testified that the cameraman was lying.

However, the more pressing issue was Lankford's suspension, additional evidence of a travesty of justice, the wounds from which the department took a long time to recover. The looming questions that remained unanswered were: why didn't the judge recuse himself? Why didn't he allow the jury to see all the evidence? How could Lankford be found guilty on such flimsy evidence? Was it because a black man had the audacity to come along and be the first one to hold such a position in the State of Georgia?

Following Lankford's suspension, in the interim, African American Robert McMichael was appointed temporary sheriff by Georgia's governor. At the time, McMichael was an investigator for the District

Attorney's office. His short tenure as sheriff was tempered by an uneasy relationship with the deputies because they'd won over his objections to our unionizing. Nonetheless, he did a very good job and ruffled no feathers.

*

The New Year, 1991, didn't begin all hale and hearty for me. The stress of the previous year began to take its toll for I found it quite unbearable to see how my mentor had been railroaded. Equally difficult during his last days was my having to hear the gossiping behind his back then see the same forked-tongue gossipers smile in his face, slap him on the back, and offer words of encouragement. I was dumbfounded! In fact, sometimes I really had to do a double-take to make sure I'd heard and seen right. Could people really be so deceptive? These were some of the same people who'd worked hard to block our unionizing and effusive in their congratulations at the musketeers' success. Now, I paused to wonder what they *really* said about me behind my back.

This I shared with Grace one day when she came to my apartment for lunch one day on my day off. She brought a KFC meal for herself, disapproving that I still ate like a bird, she said. Food was never my priority. I ate to survive, never liked to cook and did so only at gunpoint, so to speak, and was just as happy every day to have a salad and a tablespoonful of rice, as I was having then. Picking my way through my salad and rice, I gave her as much detail as necessary, trying to make light of the situation because I didn't want her to feel that anything was her fault. True, I'd relocated to Georgia at her invitation but it was my decision to follow my dream, my bliss.

Grace, biting heartily into the chicken leg, said between chews, "That's yuh problem, Maria, yuh take things to heart and hold on when yuh should let go and move on."

"People always tell me so, but that ain't true. I done walk away from many things when the time came. What yuh think have me living here and not back in Trinidad?"

"Immigrating and relocating not the same as letting go of things," she explained. "I mean you must forget. Yuh have to forget a lot of things to keep your sanity in this place. Or pretend yuh didn't see and hear what yuh know damn well you saw and heard."

"That's easier said than done, chile."

"Girlfriend, in this USofA, so yuh better make that just as easy said and done, or else yuh ain't *go* survive. Yuh understand?"

"I ain't born yesterday, yuh know, and I understand full well what it takes to survive. What I don't get is the deceitfulness. Why people can't say what they have to say to your face? Why they have to pretend everything ok then, BAM!, they slap you with something you couldn't even begin to see coming?" I pushed away the remainder of my lunch that tasted like straw now.

Grace looked at me then at my plate disapprovingly. "Doh tell me yuh kyar even finish yuh bird-meal now because yuh too upset to eat. Yuh mind?" Before I could answer, she reached with her plastic fork and helped herself to some lettuce and tomato that I hadn't touched. Crunching, she continued, "I never bother to try and understand human nature. People are people. Black people, white people, Indian people, Chinese people, all people want the same damn thing from life. To be happy. They just have different ways of getting their happiness." She sipped her Coke and continued, "The last thing I want to hear from you is that them people get the better of you. I want you to promise me that."

I laughed and said, "I know how to survive; doh worry."

She didn't return my laugh and instead insisted, "I serious fuh so, Maria. I want you to promise me that yuh doh let anybody get the best of you. Let go and move on. That's my philosophy in life."

Seeing her sober face and sensing some urgency, I simply said, "Hold strain, nuh. We's Trini women. All ah we know how to survive. Buh if yuh want me to promise, I promise."

"That's all I want to hear," she said. "Now, pass over yuh plate. Yuh know how I hate to see good food go to waste." The remainder of our lunch she spent talking about my god-daughter. How big she was getting. How she was doing in school. What she was picking up from there and from TV, and she might just have to send her back home to her grandmother for some good Trini discipline.

*

By the end of January, I decided to resign from being co-president after having been admitted to South Fulton Hospital for tests due to difficulty in breathing. The doctors initially thought that maybe I had a clot on a lung; however, the test results returned fine. I was X-rayed, lung-scanned, and blood-tested for things I didn't even know existed. Still, all results returned normal. The next day I was discharged and given a week off to rest, during which time all the symptoms disappeared.

Upon returning to work, however, all the symptoms returned with a vengeance. Difficulty in breathing. Sharp stomach pains. Vertigo in the worst way, so that I had to hold on to my desk upon rising, waiting for the world to stop spinning.

Then, one morning nothing that I ate or drank for breakfast stayed down; tomato juice, fruit cocktail, everything retched. I was off to the doctor, again, and had the strength to make it only because a tiny piece of chocolate bar stayed down. This time, my doctor discovered a bowel infection and put me on antibiotics.

While one side of my brain refused to admit that I'd developed a psychological allergic reaction to my work place, the other side clamored that I had and I must make some changes. So, I resigned from my office as co-president and accepted the realization that Helen Reddy's choir occasionally would have to exclude me. I couldn't continue to sing with gusto, "I am woman watch me grow / See me standing toe to toe."

Turning my attention to my professional development, in June I met the minimum requirements regarding my Firearm Performance Evaluation. I noted the single comment handwritten by the course instructor that I should continue to practice to achieve consistent proficiency and determined to do just that. I also welcomed my next assignment to the towers from where deputies could view the jail's activities without having to go into the inmates' area.

Previously, as co-president of our fledgling union, Sgt. Harmon and I had decided to initiate our first action on behalf of our fellow officers and make good on a promise of unionization—suing for increased wages and overtime pay. The idea that some of them had to use food stamps was unconscionable. In April, we'd organized a big protest against this, which attracted much community attention and brought TV Channels 5 and 11 to the site of the protest. Approximately twenty-one sergeants and deputies participated. Recognizing the strong show of support, we musketeers thought that a lawsuit would also have a strong show of support. Therefore, Harmon and I'd sued on behalf of everyone.

I'd allowed myself to be named on the lawsuit, even though I did not stand to benefit. I did not have enough compensation time or vacation time and never would. However, if by being named it would benefit the others, why not? I felt that I would have accomplished a milestone if we won.

We actually won!

I vowed to remember that the squeaking hinge got greased.

Bolstered by this surprising victory—a really big deal for all the deputies—I decided to lobby Interim Sheriff McMichael about the availability of water in the towers. I'd been seeing my doctor for my bowel infection that caused a recurring bladder infection due to my not drinking enough water. Everyone complained every day about there being no water, but no one did anything to rectify the situation. Taking matters into my hands, toward the end of June I mailed a complaint to the sheriff. In it, I highlighted the problem, all the verbal complaints that went unheeded, all the support of the deputies, and hence my reasons for bringing the matter to him.

My inter-office memo's subject heading was all in capital letters to accentuate my forcefulness: UNAVAILABILITY OF DRINKING WATER IN THE TOWERS. I began with stating that I'd brought up the matter at the last union meeting six months ago and was still awaiting a response. I continued by pointing out that evidently when the towers were constructed, management did not consider the importance of installing a water fountain. Hence, during an eight-hour shift, one had to go without drinking water, which was appalling especially on the days when the temperature was high. Additionally, the 3-11 shift was continuously understaffed. Therefore, if one had to relieve herself, she couldn't. The jail was staffed originally with two deputies on the floor and two in the towers. The staff was now reduced to one and one. Since neither area could be left unattended, deputies had to remain at their post regardless of their physical needs.

I wrote that I'd appealed to management and raised its awareness of this situation, to no avail. To be emphatic, I included my personal predicament: "I must drink water, and lately when I am in the towers with no one to relieve me, I have to maintain my position, and for eight hours I am without a drink of water or the privilege of exercising 'bathroom functions.' It's quite obvious that the inmates' needs are considered much more than the deputies.'" I concluded that if my appeals continued to remain unanswered, I would be left no recourse but to take the matter to higher authorities. A mild threat that was intended to state that I meant business.

After sending off the memo, I wondered whether I should have included the veiled threat. After all, no one likes to be threatened. However, when in August my appeal remained ignored and my infection returned with all its vengeful aggravations, my doctor agreed to lend his voice to the call for the availability of water—a fundamental human right—and wrote a letter to that effect. In a polite but professional tone, he stated that Ms. Pereira had been his patient for several months for a recurring bladder infection, which could be alleviated if she "drank large quantities of water throughout the day." Therefore, he recommended that potable bottle water be made available to her immediately. In early September, McMichael responded by putting bottled water in all towers. Finally!

"Well," I thought with much satisfaction, smiling as I gazed at the water, "just a little over two months. Not bad. What did we say in Trinidad? 'Grass doh grow on bottle.' Wait 'til they hear about this!" In Atlanta, the miracle of the grass-growing bottle was real, "And a woman is now walking on water, to boot." Given enough time, maybe I'd witness Jesus swimming in a river of fire, I thought in exhilaration, and the three Hebrew boys dancing in a twentieth-century furnace of fire. But had I known that by 1994 all water would be removed from the towers, I would not have gloated so much. Without such psychic vision, I was heartened by my accomplishment.

Even more bolstered, I decided the time had come to do something about the abuse of the phones. May as well try for evidence of another supernatural intervention that would shake things up. I decided to take issue with the abuse of the towers' phones that were there for jail and emergency use. The deputies completely disregarded this and, with complete lack of discretion, overdid it. Every time I turned around, all the phones were in use. I began documenting and writing them up. Consequently, the phones were disconnected. The list of my enemies began to grow for that move.

I shook my head as I reflected on how much they loved me when we won the lawsuit and the gift of water bottles, but then despised me for the unserviceable phones. I shrugged it off as evidence of that part of human nature that purred in pleasure when in comfort but growled in the gall of an inconvenience. However, I didn't realize the extent of their growing animus until early November.

CHAPTER 4 — FINDING THE SOURCE OF LIFE

The night shift on November 8, 1991 was a quiet, dull night, for which I was grateful. No drama. No incidents. The proverbial calm before the storm. I was in the tower on 3 North when suddenly the men in the TV-recreation room began pressing the buzzer incessantly. I signaled to the other deputy and asked him to go and investigate the matter.

He returned to report that he had handcuffed and removed a white inmate, Waggoner, from Zone 600 and placed him in Zone 700. He continued that approximately thirty inmates watching TV in the recreation room became animated that one of them, Jessie Lynn Waggoner, whose real name was Jessie David Baker, was that night's focus. Apparently, *America's Most Wanted* was the inmates' favorite program. They couldn't believe their eyes when they recognized one of them as that night's feature, having recognized him by his tattoos. He was wanted in Florida for killing his girlfriend. But what really excited them was the thought that they could collect the reward of one hundred thousand dollars for providing the tip for his recapture. I instructed the deputy to inform Classification and went to Zone 700 to question the inmate.

On my way, the inmates' most insistent question was whether

they'd get the reward money. I calmed them down, promising that I'd make sure they got due credit for their "work" and went to Waggoner-Baker. He was serving his sentence in Georgia for attempted robbery and rape. I got straight to the point, "Is it true that you're wanted for murder in Florida for killing your girlfriend?"

"Yeah, that's me. But I ain't kill nobody."

"What really happened, then?"

Somewhat answering the question, he said, "The reason I didn't give myself up, even though my mother told me to, was because I was afraid the system would not believe me. They're saying that I lost control when she threw me out of the house —"

I interrupted him, "Who threw you out of the house?"

"My girlfriend threw me out. And they said later, while she was sleeping, I went back inside and shot her in the head. But it wasn't me."

"Well, that's what you all say," I replied then continued, "you know that you'll have to be moved, for your own safety, while we follow up on this." He shook his head glumly, the picture of abject depression. I couldn't afford the luxury of feeling sorry for him. If I felt sorry for any one of these men, I would be most ineffective at my job. All I could offer them was the respect afforded one's fellow human beings so as not to violate their human rights. That I did evenly. Now, I simply offered what little words of consolation I could within the professional parameters and left. I went directly to Classification and spoke with the sergeant and deputy who were present, requesting that Waggoner be removed from Zone 600 for his own safety, then filled out and turned in an "Incident Report."

The next day I received a call from a lieutenant in Human Resources instructing me to be at the jail at eight o'clock the following morning. *America's Most Wanted* was coming to interview all parties concerned with the capture of the inmate wanted in Florida. The lieutenant said she was making it a point to contact and inform me because the incident happened on my floor, under my watch, and was based upon my report. She said that the others had already been contacted and it looked like they may have overlooked me, so she was personally calling to inform me.

The following morning, November 10th, a few minutes before

seven o'clock, my phone rang. Who the dickens could be calling so early? Tempted to ignore it, I, however, decided to answer. "Hello, good morning."

"Maria?"

"This is she. Oh, hi, Marlena," I said, recognizing the voice of the only friend I often felt I had left in the department.

"Girlfriend, you better get down here right now!"

"What the hell is going on now?" I asked, alarmed. Then half-jokingly, "The jail on fire, or what?"

"No! *America's Most Wanted*, the sheriff from Florida, everybody is here, and you're not. Girl, you'll be on TV!" Marlena was genuinely excited for me that I would be on national television.

"What the hell?! I was told to get there at eight, but I was planning to arrive at seven-thirty."

"Well, it looks like everyone else is here already. Sgt. Eubanks, the TV crew, everyone. So, you better hurry up and get your ass here, or you'll be shut out of *your* story."

I had just completed my video workout, showered, and was midway through dressing. With not enough time to dress as meticulously as I'd have liked, I instead quickly donned a sweater, jeans, and sneakers, grabbed my pocket-book and car keys, jumped into my car, and raced to the jail.

As I drove, I fondled my earrings that were shaped like the island of Trinidad and thought ruefully that I'd just have to keep them on. I'd planned to replace them with more professional looking ones, but without having time to do so I'd have to settle on simply putting my best smile forward for the camera, if I were to be interviewed and filmed. Oh, well.

I arrived at the lobby at approximately seven-thirty and saw Eubanks was already there but looking completely out of his element. He beckoned me to join him and together we sat and waited but with little to say to each other.

At a quarter to eight, the detective from Florida arrived. I introduced myself and asked whether he was connected with the investigation. He answered yes and in turn identified himself as Captain Cliff Miller of Putnam County Sheriff Department. While we were waiting for his pass to go up to the inmates' floor, more of the *America's Most Wanted* crew arrived. I informed them that the superintendent was on his way but they could go ahead and set up their equipment.

At approximately a quarter past eight, the superintendent arrived. I introduced everyone to him and we all went into his office. At a quarter to nine, my immediate supervisor arrived and after everyone was briefed, the superintendent gave permission for the camera crew to film on the floor. While the cameramen and jail officials went up to the floor to discuss the logistics of the filming, I remained with the superintendent but excused myself to use the Ladies' Room. I'd so rushed out the house, I wanted to check myself one last time to make sure I looked presentable.

When I returned, everyone had disappeared. I barely saw the last person disappearing into my supervisor's office. Feeling certain that he was maneuvering to take all the credit for the inmate's capture, I thought that the least he could have done was wait to hear directly from me the details of the night. I also felt that I ought to be the one interviewed first and not have to wait until he had given his incorrect version of what happened. In fact, I was very much offended when he closed the door and had me wait outside for almost an hour while he related his version.

Eventually, tired of being shafted, I went to the superintendent's office and expressed my thoughts to him. He agreed with me and told me to go and so inform my supervisor that he would have his time to be interviewed. Emboldened, I knocked on my supervisor's door and relayed the superintendent's directive. He conceded almost immediately.

When my time came, I didn't even remember what I said. Only after I received a courtesy copy of the show and viewed it, I found that I hadn't performed poorly, after all. More so, I was much relieved at the professional editing that omitted all my supervisor's erroneous details. Someone had listened and paid attention to me instead. Now that was more like the America I'd dreamt of coming to. A place where people were competent and paid attention to details. Not the joke to which some nincompoops at the F.C. Jail were reducing the institution.

Yet, I continued to be indignant that my supervisor had the nerve to try to take over completely the moment, without even giving us the option of working together to present the department's best face! What was it about some men that they felt they must hog all the glory for themselves?!

The next day, the daily carried a short article about the incident. I was not surprised but still hurt to see that my name was not even mentioned. I knew that I was not a member of the selected crowd and most likely would never be recognized by management for my diligent work. But it still was an affront the way their political machinations worked against those disfavored. I resolved, however, to continue to do my best. I was a damn good worker and to hell with them and their politics.

Nonetheless, feeling an urgency not to allow the attempts to slight my work go unaddressed, I decided to follow up with someone even higher up the chain of command and made an appointment to meet with the captain. He listened attentively as I explained what had happened. I made it clear that I was bringing the matter to his attention because I wanted to make sure that I did receive due credit for my work. He promised me a redress and that a commendation would be placed in my file. I thanked him and left, feeling better that the department was still maintaining its level of professionalism and integrity for which it was once reputed.

Some time later, however, my faith in departmental integrity once more faltered. Upon reviewing my file, as I did periodically, I noticed that no commendation letter was in my file.

*

While living in College Park, I'd resided next door to First Christian Church, a non-denominational church whose people seemed truly happy. Quite a few Sunday mornings, from the window of my apartment I'd observe their arrival and departure. The way they hugged and greeted each other seemed genuine. At least their smiles and handshakes so appeared. I wondered if those people really liked each other, and what it would be like to be in such a community, to be amongst people who were concerned about each other's well being. For many Sundays I continued to observe the folks, and how blacks, whites, Hispanics, and all mixtures seemed so happy. But the idea of sitting in a strange place for an interminable period was daunting, so

I decided to time their arrival and departure. A little over an hour. Hmm, I thought, maybe I could survive an hour.

Finally after a couple of years, I decided no longer to put off my decision to seek help from a higher power. While living in Trinidad, I'd always prayed, called on a higher power to help me through decisions that didn't seem right, or to get me out of jams. Sometimes, I'd needed help in school, or at work, or with a friendship turned sour, or fighting for what I believed was my right. However, I always returned to feeling lonely.

I'd moved from Barataria to St. James, where much social action was, because I'd lived in a part of Barataria that was more dead than alive, except for when one neighbor turned against another and resulted in a god-awful scene, the evidence of life. But for the most part, it was a sleepy East Indian neighborhood. I never regretted moving to St. James, even when things didn't work out as I expected socially. I'd fallen in love with a married man and dealt with the roller coaster of emotions such entailed. I'd left Trinidad when the opportunity presented itself. The U.S. at that time had opened up to accept another wave of immigrants from Trinidad; I'd submitted my application for a permanent visa and was excited that mine sailed through the process without a hitch. Surely, a higher power had it planned for me to immigrate.

However, I was searching for something more lasting, more satisfying in life and felt the irresistible urge to give this church a tryout. Just once to see what it was like. Timidly, I walked across the parking lot, oblivious to anything but making it to the front door without becoming too terrified to return to the safety of my apartment. Maybe the couple walking behind sensed my hesitancy, apprehension, and every unconscious vibe I emitted that spoke, "Good Lord! What the hell am I getting myself into?" They caught up to me and flanked me on both sides with an effervescent greeting.

"Well, hello there! Good morning! How're ya doing on this fine Lord's day?"

"Beautiful day, ain't it?"

"I don't think I've seen ya before. Is this ya first time?"

"Come on in. We love first-timers."

"I'm Sally Rivers."

"And, I'm Billy Rivers[5]. Our children are visiting their grandparents this weekend, so it's just the two of us. This morning only."

"We're a friendly people here. Really."

All of which came without their pausing for my response. I smiled into his grey-blue eyes and her light brown ones. They simply and quite literally embraced me and invited me to sit with them. I was most grateful for company with which to enter the building and sanctuary, which appeared to seat comfortably approximately five hundred people. I barely managed to eke out my mumbled responses and follow them meekly to a pew on the left of the sanctuary.

I loved the choruses, hymns, the short sermon, and best of all that the offering plate came around only once. I was stringently saving for a house and couldn't afford any lavish offering. I'd brought with me a single five-dollar note, having determined that that was all I was willing to give as a first-time visitor. I'd heard from my black girlfriends who attended black churches that sometimes the offering plate was passed two and three times. The pastor collected his due. The special speaker, when there was one, collected his due. Then the church collected its due for whatever special project was underway, and there was *always* a special project. I was happy that this church's one collection apparently satisfied all needs.

At the end of the service, both Sally and Billy hugged me and asked whether I enjoyed the service. With genuine sincerity, I responded that I did and hoped to return.

"Wonderful!" the cheerful couple rejoined and introduced me to the folks milling around nearby.

After shaking hands, smiling till my cheeks hurt, and promising to return, I walked out of the building into the beautiful sunlight of the day. I felt all warm and glowing inside. There was a good spirit in that place, I thought. I also could bet and win that these neighbors would not kill each other over opposing gods. I really got the feeling that they were a live-and-let-live people who simply enjoyed people. All people, regardless of race, color, or gender. What a difference!

After attending for more than a year, I felt the tug to surrender my heart and life to Jesus. To be born again. One morning, in response to the pastor's call to be saved, and during the singing of the hymn

---

5   Not their real names.

"I Surrender All," I quietly slipped out of my seat and made my way down the aisle to the front, just as I'd seen dozens do. Bowing my head, I repeated the prayer of confession and felt warmly at peace. I knew that this was the right step to make in my life. No more searching for peace. I now had the Prince of Peace living within. No more desire for comfort. The Source of Comfort, the Comforter was mine to claim. And no more uncertainty regarding my future, both in the present and the hereafter. The Wonderful Counselor was always already presenting my case before the Father and arguing in my defense. No more disappointing outcomes, either. My case was always already won, despite the outcome.

CHAPTER 5 — LIFE BENEATH THE SURFACE

Interim Sheriff McMichael continued to do an excellent job in everyone's opinion, and the tension between him and the deputies abated. Further, he was a respectable family man, and it was obvious to everyone that he understood what his staff members wanted, which was to be able to provide for their own families. His respect for everyone was equitable and without favoritism, his sense of fairness evident even in regard to his daughter, a deputy. She received no preferential treatment and had to go through seniority as did everyone else. Therefore, she worked the late-night 11-7 shift and received week days off, similarly to everyone else. Everyone was grateful for his fair leadership.

I appreciated that my own assignment in the towers. It was a position that demanded two deputies who maintained a constant vigil, kept the doors locked at all times, and didn't leave their post until their shift was over. This was why, when I was first assigned there, I didn't join in the chorus of complainers about there being no drinking water, and got down to brass tacks of writing Sheriff McMichael and calling attention to the problem.

Most likely due to my bold initiative to write this letter, I was, however, unaware that McMichael had begun keeping a close record of my leadership skills and had decided to give me the opportunity to develop further my potential. Having sensed a growing animosity toward me, I'd decided to keep my head ducked low by minding my own business, executing my duties to the best of my abilities by being conscientious and attentive to all details, and treating everyone with equanimity, due respect, and fairness. One day, he invited me into his office.

I was pleasantly surprised and honored to learn that I was being given the opportunity to attend the Jail Management Training course being offered in Colorado but offered by the University of Kentucky, all expenses paid. He appreciated my work ethics and dedication to the department and had confidence that my potential equaled that of upper management, on par with a lieutenant or a warden. I was the first sergeant to be so esteemed. To prove that I qualified, I had to write an essay describing my career goals. In my essay, I included my main career objective—to be the first West Indian female to attain the position of Captain. I was delighted that I qualified and was one among thirty-five law enforcement upper management people from all over the country. We attended a week-long class, graduated with a certificate and the extra credits certification afforded, and trained to speak publicly. A part of our training entailed class members interviewing each other.

Meanwhile, the election to fill the sheriff's position was imminent. Two were in competition for the position: McMichael and Lankford's former chief administrative officer, Jacqueline Barrett. To better place herself in competition for the position, she snagged a job in the training center. Additionally, she secured Lankford's endorsement, which made it a bit of a challenge for McMichael to win the 1993 election without much of a fight.

Admittedly, I did not vote for Barrett but still visited her office, congratulated her, and gave her what was regarded as an initial letter opener that stated my respect for her and the expectation of working well with her. It was my first direct contact with her and I must say that the visit went better than I expected, for she was pleasant, diplomatic, but brusquely professional. She was a rather plain-looking African American woman, about my height and size. She commented that she'd thought I was taller than she found me when we stood up to shake hands at the conclusion of our meeting.

Despite her professional demeanor, as I left I couldn't shake off the uneasy feeling I had about her. She didn't strike me as being intimidated by anything or anyone, and certainly not by the likes of me. So, what was it? I guess I'd just have to wait and see, I reassured myself, and hoped that I was wrong.

You see, I preferred McMichael; certainly, he was an excellent choice for the job. He'd proved to be a decent man with impeccable morals, a professional who dealt with those under his command fairly though not always diplomatically, and best of all, was not chasing after every woman simply because he could. That was something I couldn't say of the other ranking male officers, some of whom were married.

Without allowing that brand of social politics to assert undue influence upon me, I focused instead on the round of course-work that had once more descended upon me. Hitting the books in conjunction with perfect attendance at all the courses paid off. In March, I received my training certificate from Georgia Women in Law Enforcement. This was followed by my Certificate of Achievement of Continuing Education Units from Eastern Kentucky University. I was, by dint of hard work and education, doing my best to prepare for mobility up the ranks and had arrived at the mid-level managerial position.

Still, there was one critical lesson I had to learn. More accurately, I still had to be tested by fire and survive, like those three Hebrew boys in Nebuchadnezzar's furnace. I also still had to figure out how to remain sharp.

Long ago in ancient China, there lived a Chinese cook who never needed to sharpen his knife, while all the other cooks had to constantly sharpen theirs or purchase new ones.

One day, the old, wise master chef came to visit, and carefully observed the young cooks—all his former apprentices—as they cut their meats to prepare the dinner meal. He smiled as he observed the only one who was using the same knife he had been given years ago as an apprentice. He observed that he'd remembered how to cut around the visible bones and find the bones that lay deeply hidden within the carcass. Instead of first plunging his knife in, he reached his hand carefully inside and located the path along which his

knife must travel. The old, wise chef smiled again and gamboled
away as light-footed as a deer.
Back in his village, his wife wished to know why he was so happily
dancing around and making her dizzy.
"My wife," he paused his dancing and replied, "one young student
has not forgotten my lesson."
"Which one is that?"
Laughing heartily he said, "The one who understood best that to
remain sharp and precise she must always follow the path of least
resistance." He chuckled and continued, "All the others are well on
their way to becoming dull."

At the time of the election in 1992, I'd returned to being co-president of the union and decided upon a solution to the predicament of electing the next sheriff, the election that resulted in Barrett's winning. I'd recommended that the executive board call for a debate between the two contenders. A debate would've allowed everyone to see which of the two would make a better sheriff. The matter was particularly sensitive and had to be resolved as amicably as possible. Surprisingly, McMichael had angered some of the deputies by calling them inadequate—not at all diplomatic—so they were happy to see him go.

I, however, was unsympathetic toward their anger. After all, I'd observed that some high ranking officers could not even write a simple incident report yet were promoted. What were *their* qualifications? Hence, I thought that a debate would've allowed everyone to judge the competency of the two candidates, which I'd thought was fair. Much to my dismay, some deputies registered in no uncertain terms their adamant position against the debate idea and voted for the union to nominate Barrett.

I guess that I was not the only one to pay the price for speaking the truth to power. Some people—irrespective of race or ethnicity—didn't duck low, or play ball, or sit on the fence. They called a spade a spade and suffered the consequences. Like me.

Needless to say, with the backing of the majority of the union members, Barrett became the first African American female sheriff in the country. I, on the other hand, was snubbed by some members of the union's executive board because I'd openly supported McMichael. Resistance to my every endeavor intensified thereafter, and my every goal was tested by fire. The fact that I'd presented in writing my acceptance of the election's outcome and willingness to move forward positively did not weigh sufficiently in my favor. Animosity toward me continued to grow and one way I survived was returning frequently to the more pleasant—and some ambivalent—memories of Trinidad.

*

Indo-Trinidadians learned to navigate their colonial space with much social skill and aplomb for what they had already contributed to the nation. East Indians were the second largest racial group of the country, the largest being those of African descent who comprised about forty-five percent of the population, with the East Indians comprising approximately forty percent, and the remainder of Europeans, Middle Easterners, and Chinese descent. There was also a growing minority of those who had intermarried and produced multiracial children, who in turn were intermarrying and bringing into existence many beauties like Janelle Commissiong, Wendy Fitzgerald, and Tatiana Ali; those who excelled in cricket like Brian Lara and in Track and Field like Ato Boldon and Hasley Crawford; those whose vocals are second to none like Heather Headley, Denise Plummer, Singing Sandra, and David Rudder; scholars and writers like C. L. R. James, V. S. Naipaul, and Earl Lovelace; and comedian Paul Keens Douglas, whose descriptive of Tanty Merle on Carnival Day was right on par with Bill Cosby's Fat Albert.

Trinidadians, since before the country's Independence in 1962, had begun to appreciate and delight in each other's diversity. Such delight was apparent especially during lunch time, when lunches were furtively swapped because an East Indian girl preferred her African classmate's *pelau*; or the African preferred her East Indian one's curried *channa* and rice; or the dougla preferred the European girl's sandwiches that were neatly trimmed of the ends and cut diagonally; or the European girl smacked her lips at her dougla friend's *mauby* and *accra*. Then came Independence and lunches could be openly shared because the National Anthem sang of celebrating the equality of every creed and race. These girls of the sixties and seventies boasted of enjoying the most cosmopolitan society of the Western Hemisphere, some cognizant that in a few years they could teach to get along people who lived in countries whose thin veneer of peace was constantly threatened by the underlying tensions of racism.

Even beyond Trinbagonians' growing acceptance of their unique place in the Caribbean, they especially prided themselves in Carnival, the season when all lingering differences miraculously vanished. On every Carnival Monday and Tuesday, the people who participated blended into a sea of variegated, pulsating unity, dancing rhythmically throughout the streets of Port of Spain to steelband music as they paraded in respective *mas* (masquerade) bands.

Who weren't members of a mas band enjoyed the foods of the various vendors selling every imaginable curry dish: curried potato with curried goat, beef, chicken, or chick peas to fill the *roti*. Other vendors enticed spectators and revelers, Trinbagonians and tourists alike, with *pelau, callaloo* and crab, rice and peas, sweet bread, *accra*, sugar-cake, peanut brittle, *channa, toulum, palowri*, and *doubles*. All these finger-licking edibles were washed down with *mauby, sorrel*, ginger-beer, rum-and-coke, *pina colada*, sweet drink, Carib Lager beer, or any concoctions of an anonymous drink-maker.

Some Trinbagonians, like me, preferred Carnival Monday for the mas bands. I used to work diligently throughout the pre-season beading costumes for the mas band for whom Invaders Steel Band played. Beading meant many sleepless nights and sore fingers and thumbs. But I loved it! Even after being disheartened when Birdie Mannette dragged my work through the streets because he became too drunk to wear his costume properly. Every year, I still beaded for him and all the other masqueraders.

What an incredible display of the aesthetic and imagination by artistic-band-costume designers such as Peter Minshall, George Bailey, and others! One band's theme was "Birds of Paradise," while another's was "Buccoo Reef," or another, "Glorious Tropical Sunset," names in those days that celebrated all the splendid beauty of the Caribbean. All masqueraders paraded a kaleidoscopic array of costumes that literally exploded the brilliant and subtle colors and hues of the rainbow. The highlight of all bands was the most spectacular king and queen who brought up the rear of the band and were never a disappointment. Like ancient, godly royalty, these kings and queens bore costumes that spanned in breadth possibly twenty-four feet and in height possibly twelve to eighteen feet of intricate designs and colors even more breathtaking than their subjects. The evidence of such imagination always thrilled me.

During Carnival season, Trinbagonians didn't wonder why the European empire-builders left their respective ancestors in the lands of their origin. Such grouching was for a time when things weren't going the way the people thought they should, which occurred frequently outside the Carnival season. Politically-minded and academic Trinbagonians discussed how the wicked dragged people half-way around the world from Africa, India, and China and dumped them on different islands they didn't know a thing about among people they didn't know a thing about, then rewarded and punished according to their rules that were constantly changing faster than the Ganges, Indus, or Nile flowed even on their worst flood days. It was more than enough to keep anyone from suffering constantly from vertigo and feeling that vertigo was natural and disequilibrium the state of the universe. How the blazes were people supposed to know which was the right path to follow without missing a step because they were so constantly off-balance?

Then, Basdeo Panday came into power and made a lot of East Indians ashamed to be Trinbagonians for the wanton display of racism that some Indians borrowed from the United States and Britain. Are people's memories so short that they could so easily forget that not so long ago, less than a generation, Trinbagonians prided themselves in the country's unofficial watchword, "All ah we is one," or in the National Anthem whose theme boasted that in Trinidad and Tobago every Jack and Jill found equality and parity? A boast not quite born out in reality even back then because Behind the Bridge and St. Clair existed on lines of socio-economic latitude that never converged or intersected. Still, the pretense that the degrees of separation vanished on Carnival days kept Trinbago society from swirling off its axis of political order. More concretely, an uneasy tension resided among some East Indians and Africans who didn't hesitate to refer to each other derogatively privately or publicly as good-for-nothing *niggers* or curry-smelling *coolies*.

Without refutation and apparently oblivious to racial chasms, during the late sixties to early seventies an alarming wave of suicide among East Indian teenage girls arose among those who refused to live without their Negro boyfriends with whom they'd fallen in love but were forbidden by their parents to see. So, resigning themselves to love's precariousness, these parents relented and allowed their daughters to follow love's dictate. Otherwise, they faced the reality that these heart-broken daughters loved in an unfathomable way. These daughters, whose love couldn't be circumscribed by racial or familial codes of conduct, chose to die in order to make that statement reverberate across the land. Surely, these parents felt their world was spinning out of control, too, but they helped to bring stability to an environment into which they themselves eased uneasily.

*

Living in Georgia, I had become familiar with vertigo, and to deal with it I'd learned to pray, "Lord, help me. Lord, help us all along this journey we call life." Meanwhile, I grew in confidence that I'd always followed my heart, which, I was the first to say, had been often deceptive when I was less experienced and had led to some bad behavior. Some of such I chose constantly to put out of my mind. Let the sleeping dogs of Trinidad—and their dreams, too—lie, grow old, then die. No need regretting the past, either. What happened, happened. The present that shaped the future was what mattered.

CHAPTER 6 — FORGING CONNECTIONS

In January of 1993, I became a member of an ad hoc committee formed to amend the "Lock Out Policy," my voice representing the department's policies. The committee had been formed to address the growing concerns that an overpopulated jail posed a threat to everyone's—inmates and staff alike—safety. It was one of the most efficient committees on which I worked during my entire tenure. In one day we completed our evaluation and recommendation and submitted it to the superintendent. He, in turn, was so impressed that he thanked us personally and decided to adopt our suggested amendment as standard policy.

The memorandum read (replicated here verbatim):

•

Policy: At 0500 hours, the Inmates in general population will come off lock-in. The doors will remain in complete open position at all times, until the 2300 hour headcount is completed.

This excludes 2 South, 3 South (400 & 500 zones) and 7 North.

[The list of Procedures included 7 items that detailed exactly what was to be done during the lock-in/lock-out duration.]

Exception: If both Inmates in a particular cell have been loaned out (Court, Grady, etc.) that cell door will be secured and this information will be reflected in the tower (log books and panel).

Pros:

Doors unlocked between the 0500 hour and the 2300 hour will serve the purpose of:
1. Safety and security of Staff and Inmates by minimizing the number of Inmates in the dayroom area.

2. To reduce tension.

3. To provide easy access to jail services:
a. Medication
b. Mail
c. Visitation
d. Commissary

4. Reduces damage to locks and other jail property

5. Sanitation and hygienic reasons.

All six of us members of the committee felt proud of our work, too. We all looked forward to a positive change that would enhance the safety of both staff and inmates.

*

Later that year in May, 1993, the sensation of the department was Barrett being featured on PBS's *To the Contrary* for its focus on women in dangerous jobs, in high-risk professions, a taping that included me as one of the two hundred plus women deputies on the job. The State of Georgia had been abuzz with the distinction of having elected the first African American woman in the country at the helm of the law enforcement ship. Consequently, not only feminists were taking pride in this "first," so were black women. I, in particular, felt quite hopeful that a black woman in headship would make life a little easier for women in law enforcement. We were all proud of her accomplishment, regardless of her politicking to earn the spot. We were so very hopeful that a woman who understood what it was like to be discriminated against and oppressed would not become a partner in the oppression of women.

The department went to some lengths to prepare for the PBS cameras, which paid off because the filming went without a hitch. My partner and I were featured on our rounds, and two other female deputies were featured manhandling the men, some of them hardened criminals.

When I received my copy of the video, I was proud of the entire department and of the women in particular. Barrett's comments were especially striking. She spoke of how pleased she was to be distinguished as the first black woman sheriff in the country, and how she didn't place her work over her family whose members were quite supportive of her demanding duties that entailed seven hundred deputies under her supervision. I was heartened to hear her acknowledge that female deputies trained as rigorously as the males to prepare for their jobs, and that she was proud of females in law enforcement. She pointed out that they brought to the position "cooler heads, tended to follow the rules, created a safer environment, yet they didn't shirk tough assignments."

But I took particular interest in the comment that she would try to open up opportunities for women to advance, which shouldn't be hard because the female deputies were well trained, exercised common sense, and were tremendous assets to law enforcement, she boasted. I was soon to learn that Barrett intended to employ her own brand of politics that didn't embrace all blacks. Barrett was yet another same old-same old politician who didn't hesitate to use the "you-stroke-my-back-and-I'll-stroke-yours" philosophy when dealing with everyone. This became evident in 1994 with the water bottles.

Prior to their removal, it became evident that a new type of laxity was emerging. First, people began smoking in unauthorized areas, which caused me some consternation so I lodged a written complaint. I was, after all, allergic to cigarette smoke—as noted in my file—and thought everyone was aware of the dangers of second-hand smoke. Surely, I was acting in the best interest of everyone's health by calling attention to the violation. However, I received no response to the complaint.

Next, one day I observed a male deputy escorting an inmate from the floor to an office. Shortly afterward, I heard singing coming from the office. Upon investigation, I discovered that two sergeants were being entertained by an inmates' choir, of sorts. A concert was in progress, if you please! When I questioned one sergeant about the concert, he said it was the other sergeant's idea. I wrote this one up, also, this time copying it to the captain. To this memorandum, the sheriff responded by warning all members of the department that should such fraternization occur, it would be the grounds for serious disciplinary action.

Then, I found that I had to address, by way of reminder, a breakdown in the processing of inmates. I wanted to nip in the bud some infractions that could become standard, the most grievous ones being: the flow and quantity of inmates in the sallyport area that threatened the maintenance of security; some deputies entering the jail with their weapons; female inmates not being separated from male ones; male deputies frisking female inmates; some inmates' possessions not being searched very thoroughly for contraband; and, the control station not kept secured because the door to the Control Tower was always open. Whenever I reported to relieve the deputy on duty, I closed the door. However, as soon as I left, the next deputy opened the door and kept it open. Such was a grave breach of security.

Another serious breach was a female deputy who refused to wear her gun when assigned to an armed post. I pointed out to her that whenever she was in uniform she was to wear her gun, which was a part of the uniform. She insolently responded that she left it at home. I wrote a memo to the lieutenant drawing his attention to this serious infraction and stating that the next time this deputy reported to an armed post without her weapon, I would write her up and request disciplinary action be taken. Did these deputies think they were working with candy-stealers, or what? Some inmates were hard-core criminals who wouldn't hesitate to beat the living daylights out of a deputy!

Despite my concerted efforts to adhere to department policy, by August of that year I felt that things were spiraling out of control, dangerously so. I began to keep a list of violations and my efforts to arrest inappropriate and unacceptable behavior:

the loud playing of radios

smoking in non-permitted areas

allowing doors to remain open that should be kept closed, which ran the risk of prisoners' escape

eating and drinking while using the computers, which, in the event of spills, damaged the keyboards and consequently caused unnecessary costs to the tax-payers

eating in the control intake area and listening to loud rap music

leaving the building to purchase food and attend to other private matters

civilian workers having access to keys that they should not have access to

important keys being misplaced or lost

leaving one's shift in complete chaos.

When I proceeded to submit these violations in writing, I was moved to another area. In fact, the pattern emerged that when I complained about infractions in any area, I was moved to another. In this way, I was constantly being moved. Nevertheless, some employees complimented me for my diligence. The telephone operator was especially grateful for the restoration of quiet, which allowed her finally to hear the person on the other end of the phone line.

I was appalled to see that the accelerating breakdown was happening under a woman's watch. Surely, when McMichael was at the helm he ran a tighter ship, and the removal of the water bottles after his departure in 1994 literally and symbolically signaled the drying up of generosity and kindness. Shortly thereafter, the phones were reconnected but for a limited time only.

I wondered at the lesson to be learned from water bottles and phones.

Barrett's true colors began to emerge without disguise the following year.

*

The year 1995 began excitedly.

During all of January, I anticipated my February trip to Melbourne, Australia, with Sgt. Fronie Buffington, a trip whose expenses we ourselves underwrote. Fronie, who was white and about my height and size, worked at the Court House, which was where we met when I was a member of the Honor Guard. The Honor Guard was a special unit of the Sheriff Department, whose members were trained to march and perform at parades and funerals and special occasions.

I had tried unsuccessfully to gain funding for an F. C. County Sheriff Department's delegation to participate in the 1995 World Police and Fire Games. However, the department claimed its budget could not afford to send anyone. Not to be deterred, Fronie and I then decided to pay our own way. It was worth it! We refused to allow this opportunity to slip by, especially since I'd receive a letter of invitation from the president of the games. I was so excited when the invitation came that I'd drafted a proposal for a delegation and submitted both the letter and proposal to Barrett. I'd prayed that Barrett would approve it. To my dismay, Barrett regretfully denied it, claiming lack of sufficient funds.

I noted that ironically in '93 and '94 Barrett and her chosen ones attended the National Organization for Black Law Enforcement (NOBLE). NOBLE convened at a different part of the country annually, and was attended by the same individuals whose expenses were fully covered by department funds. Yet, there was no money for a delegation to the Melbourne games. I finally realized that it was useless trying to accomplish anything that was not on the sheriff's agenda and resolved never to ask anything of her. Ever. With that determination, I'd decided to pay my own way to the games and was glad that I did.

One highlight was being able to spend a few hours at the Victoria Police Academy where I distributed International Association of Women Police (IAWP) applications to officers from other countries and encouraged them to join. From that meeting, Fronie and I made

57

many new friends in law enforcement from all over the world. Forty-six countries participated in the games. In all, approximately seven thousand competitors and participants—some with their families—were in attendance. Personally, I was able to visit with some of my own relatives who lived in Melbourne.

Upon my return, I completed my required "Supervisor In-Service" course work.

*

During rare moments, I paused to reflect upon my accomplishments, at my age. Any young person who groused about how hard education was, I'd have them know that I stood in a long line of fifty-plus-year-old men and women who refused to allow age to be a deterrent factor to success.

Maybe, my own daughter would take heart and give herself that extra push, too. I've never regretted allowing Lynn to return home for recovery after any fall. A mother was always a mother and could never turn her back on her child. Nevertheless, I still had little patience for those of the younger generation who were full of excuses for their own failures. Life in America has not been easy for anyone, particularly black women who remained at the bottom of society's socio-economic hierarchy. But, I imagined, everyone, including the filthy rich, awoke every day and made choices, for better or worse, and then lived with the consequences. *C'est la vie.*

At my age, now in the middle fifties, I was still a slim five-six in dress-size and very attractive. Under my sheriff's hat, I wore my naturally black, straight hair with naturally gentle waves at shoulder length. Whether in my officer's uniform or in plain clothes, I was aware that men of all ages and races still turned to look at me as I walked by, feigning unawareness of their stares. I knew that if I smiled ever so slightly to any of my lustful co-workers, single or married, they would line up to "sample the goods," as they referred demeaningly to easy women, or those who used sex to buy favors.

The idea of prostituting myself for an occasional extra day off wasn't worth entertaining for even one moment. What I had to offer was worth much more than a day or two off. For my part, they could

58

keep all extras—days off and anything else—to themselves. My manner spoke clearly to all and sundry, "Classification: Way out of your reach." I know; I thought quite highly of myself. Why shouldn't I? If I didn't, who would? Besides, a woman commanded as much respect as she had in herself. I was certain to radiate that I respected myself highly. The thought of trading favors for days off was so ludicrous that I was appalled that any female deputy consented to such devaluation. For my part, I would remain quite contented with my Mondays and Tuesdays days off, a schedule I'd had since prior to my promotion in 1988, and hoped that I would be a good example to the female deputies who were hired after I was. I wanted those who felt pressured to compromise know that they could maintain their integrity and not be like those who grinned, flirted, or plainly degraded themselves for weekends off. And weekends off to do what?

It wasn't long before I realized exactly what they did and that some of the young female deputies had questionable morals. One day while working the jail floor with a couple of them, some of the male prisoners recognized them as strippers. Listening to their raucous, disrespectful language made me feel morally repulsed. It never ceased to dismay me that so many young women continued to ignore how low they degraded themselves in others' eyes. Would such young women recognize that to have common criminals see them as nothing meant they were being regarded as nothing but pond scum? When I realized, however, that these young hussies didn't even blush in shame or embarrassment, I decided to shrug them off myself. Still, I could not help but blush for them. When it became obvious that these strippers had absolutely no authority over the prisoners, and the absence of authority posed a grave discipline problem, the prisoners were moved to a different area. What a travesty! The keepers of civil order had absolutely no moral or social leg on which to stand to enforce this order. Is this what society had come to?

Afterwards, I could not help but wonder what pimp hired them in the first place, for he must have been a pimp. It couldn't have been McMichael; he was above that. The incident also gave me pause to speculate on the extent to which the dynamics of the department had changed under a boss whom I'd rightly—which was how I felt at that moment—voted against.

I soon began to lose hope that some good would come of having a new sheriff at the helm, and a female one at that. Still, I dared to hope against hope whenever I visited Barrett in her downtown office that she would clamp down on the womanizing male officers. Having to go downtown was the first change Barrett had brought to her new position. Whereas McMichael had his office at the jail, Barrett opted to have her office at the Court House. And hers was quite posh, too, in contrast to the jail offices. What did they say? With rank comes privilege. Obviously, some people knew how to claim then abuse privilege, as I continued to learn the hard way.

MVP AWARD

MARIA PEREIRA
FULTON COUNTY SHERIFF DEPARTMENT

has been awarded the honor and title

Most Valuable Person

In recognition of hard work and outstanding leadership , and by
recommendation of employees on the Three to Eleven Shift Jail
Division. Voted Deputy Sergeant of The Year.

Presented this 3rd day of December 1999

Signed
JOHN EUBANKS
Watch Commander

The Government of

Fulton County, Georgia

Awards this Certificate to

Maria Pereira

in Recognition and Appreciation of

15

*Years of Dedicated Public Service
rendered as a County Employee*

_____
CHAIRMAN, BOARD OF COMMISSIONERS

August, 2000

Fulton County Sheriff's Department
Jacquelyn H. Barrett, Sheriff

Gregory P. Henderson
Chief Deputy

Caudell Jones
Chief Jailer

Burt F. Kamin
Chief of Staff

Justice Center Tower, 9th Floor
185 Central Ave., S.W.
Atlanta, Georgia 30303
(404) 730-5100

August 17, 2000

Sergeant Maria Pereira
Fulton County Sheriff's Department
185 Central Avenue
Atlanta, Georgia 30303

Dear Sergeant Pereira:

It is my distinct pleasure to congratulate you on fifteen years of service with the Fulton County Government and the Sheriff's Department. Speaking for the entire department, I would like to thank you for your commitment, your dedication to the citizens we serve, and contributions you have made as part of this team. As you know, the effectiveness of any organization can be no greater than the team that serves it.

I look forward to your continuing to be a very viable and valuable part of this department.

Sincerely,

Jacquelyn H. Barrett

Jacquelyn H. Barrett

JHB:csr

This photo is taken on May 24, 2000 in 6 S Sgt office. This is a TV?

Chapter 7 — Ray of Light

As one who was allergic to cigarette smoke, I very rarely made physical rounds in the day rooms where the prisoners were allowed to smoke. After I was promoted in 1988, my responsibility was to assign the deputies under my charge and make sure they completed their rounds and kept the area secure. This I did diligently, being careful not to give Cpt. Caudell Jones any reason to criticize me. Jones, nonetheless, constantly harassed me for not making rounds in the day rooms. But that was a cover. He was piqued because I rebuffed his sexual overtures. I had to; just the thought of him touching me was revolting, and not because he'd betrayed us when we were unionizing. Nor was it because he was African American because my ex-husband was half black; I'd chased after a married man who was a multi-racial black, as was my best friend, Grace. As a newborn Christian, I found it morally reprehensible that a married man with children behaved like he was foot-loose and fancy-free. In retaliation to my disdain, he used every opportunity to make my life uncomfortable, turning on its head the saying, "Hell hath no fury like a woman scorned." After complaining about his behavior to the chief who did nothing about it, I decided to take my grievance to the sheriff.

That day as I was leaving Barrett's office, I ran into Chief Briggs, the new chief jailer, who was also visiting Barrett. Chief Brownlee had retired, and few chiefs had come and gone before Briggs, a Barrett groupie, took up residence, so to speak. My heart plunged. After Barrett's election in 1993, she'd promoted to unclassified positions the two sergeants in the union who'd openly supported her. Others who'd secretively supported McMichael later easily secured her good favor because they kept their heads low. I couldn't and didn't. I'd been too open and honest in my support of McMichael and apparently was paying dearly for my "crime." In my new position, I was at the mercy of Briggs who despised me for my documenting and reporting. He proceeded to harass me, first by changing my days off, then by constantly rotating my assignments. I patiently bore this, too, and held firmly to the belief that justice will prevail.

Seeing him visit Barrett, I was sure that she would say something to him because the two were as thick as thieves. So far, nothing much had changed under Barrett's watch; in fact, the behavior of the male predators had worsened. It was no secret that high ranking officers were sleeping with several deputies. However, Briggs's animosity didn't follow a similar path.

Briggs hated my guts, as he often told me with open rancor, because I was a stickler to Policy and Procedure who believed that I was more Christian than Christ himself and morally superior to all of them. He thus felt it was his purpose in life to teach me to play ball, so to speak, and be a team-player. I, however, dismissed the jibe at my Christian beliefs and I simply saw myself as someone who couldn't and didn't know how to look the other way. Hadn't I learned when I'd injured my hand and didn't follow Policy and Procedure that laws were made to be adhered to? No, what I was doing was protective not only of myself but everyone, and it had nothing to do with my Christianity.

Thus, when he repeatedly ordered me to stop sending copies of complaints to the sheriff, I ignored him. In exasperation, he announced that not only did the sheriff have better things to do, she didn't need to be reminded of her job. She, like all of them, knew her job and didn't need someone like me to tell her or any of them what to do. In response, I'd calmly stated that maybe some people didn't know their job because if they did my complaints would be unnecessary. I continued that instead of trying to fault me for looking out for everyone's best interest he should be saying thank you. If looks could kill, as we said back home, I would have dropped dead at the look he gave me. He muttered something indistinguishable and strode off without waiting for anything further I might have said.

That night, I prayed for extra strength, as I sensed that if he could he'd do his best to kick me to the curb.

The next day, he began moving me from one area to another, making sure he kept me out of the reception area where I could observe the ins and outs of those who held two jobs. It was no secret that one captain clocked in, then left the jail and went to work at another job, while still on the County clock, then returned and signed out as though he'd been at the jail the entire day. This captain's deputy slept most of the day in the reception room. Others shirked their duties and remained hassle-free because they were in the thick with Barrett. Now, my wave of harassment had begun simply because I was not.

Frustrated at being constantly harassed and criticized for nothing, I decided to begin filing grievances. Nothing like a paper trail to protect oneself. I soon learned, however, that all my grievances were simply dismissed. Since such was the case, I requested a transfer to the Court House. The next thing I learned from an announcement on the bulletin board was that three newly promoted sergeants were transferred to the Court House. With a sinking feeling in the pit of my stomach and a bitter taste in my mouth, I realized that my request was completely ignored. Upon inquiring, I was informed that the sheriff had made those transfers. When I pointed out my seniority and that I should have received one of the three transfers, I was told that even though I had the experience and seniority, such did not matter.

Not being content with that explanation, I filed another grievance. By this time, I had developed the reputation of being a trouble-maker among those who'd voted for the sheriff. They dubbed me "The foreigner," and most of them stopped speaking to me. They accused me of not being a follower and wanting only to be a leader. However, I ignored it all and continued to perform my work exceptionally well, making sure no one could criticize my job performance.

I made sure that I was never late, that I showed all due respect to those in authority, as well as those under my command, and made it known that most of all I feared only God, not any man or woman. Though I never wore my religion, politics, or heart on my sleeve, everyone knew that I was a conservative Republican and Christian. I believed in honesty and integrity, which apparently some of my co-workers lacked. My moral standards spoke volumes without my having to say a word, and for that I was never a part of their circles, inner or otherwise. Even though a few other deputies were aware of my growing trials by fire, they were scared to do or say anything. Bootlicking, I recognized as their behavior, and bore them no grudges or resentment.

I was also aware that nepotism plagued the department. Everyone was everyone's cousin how many times removed. While County regulation did not encourage nepotism, no one did anything to prevent or stop it from exacerbating. Hence, one had to be careful of one's words. A cousin was always listening.

All I could do was pray for change and that my own situation would improve. God surely answered my prayer just when I thought I was at breaking point.

The sheriff ordered one of her female appointed majors, Major Horne, to speak with me. Following our talk, Horne offered me a job in which she would be my boss and I could choose my hours; additionally, even though the office was in the basement, I would be out of Briggs's way. Adequately placated, I accepted Horne's offer and halted the last grievance, grateful that I had a new assignment.

My new job was fine and for the first time in weeks I looked forward to going to work. It wasn't too long, though, before a cloud appeared to darken my sunny position.

Some deputies who were the sheriff's cronies had grown accustomed to doing as they pleased, with the sheriff looking the other way. Basking in the glow of her favoritism and confident that they could get away with insubordination toward me, they defiantly disobeyed my orders. After I wrote them up for insubordination, they bragged that I would get nowhere with it. How right they were! Before I could blink twice, once more *I* was being reassigned. All I could do was wait for blind Lady Justice to weigh them all in the balances then let her gavel drop. Little did I know that 1996 would bring the first call to reckoning.

While awaiting Lady Justice, I was grateful for the union and its power to defend and protect me from unfair treatment. With the strength of its power, I was able, on the day that the chief jailer threatened me with dismissal, to assert to his retreating back, "You know, you cannot chase me away from my job. In fact, you will leave before I do. You just wait and see!" I'd yelled the last sentence, to which he waved his dismissal of my prescience without turning around. Words spoken in bravado, I'd no idea how prophetic I was being. In fact, I was genuinely amazed when eventually Barrett fired him.

However, Barrett was compelled to clean shop. On the one hand, as sheriff, she was instrumental in helping provide law enforcement for the 1996 Summer Olympic Games. On the other hand, she was faced with an $812,000 "reverse discrimination" lawsuit, filed by sixteen white Fulton County deputy sheriffs—their response to her "I'm the HNIC"[6] attitude. She hadn't even tried to erect a façade of equity that would have lolled the department into a false sense of security under a female sheriff. She had gone straight into demolition derby mode and ruined all the goodwill fostered through Lankford's fair and just treatment and maintained by McMichael, for the most part. The sixteen litigants were able to provide substantial evidence of discrimination in promotions, transfers, assignments, and discipline. A federal court jury ruled fairly in their favor and awarded them full damages. Lady Justice ruled!

Barrett had no choice but to fire all the deputies whom she'd promoted to unclassified positions and were not members of the union, and others who were not qualified. Briggs fell into one of those categories. To compensate for the firings, Barrett had to remove jail deputies and place them in these vacated positions, which left the jail under-staffed and lacking adequate security.

*

She'd abused her authority and it hadn't taken long for her to slip and slide down the muddy road she'd made. She'd flaunted democratic ideals by reducing them to an absurd farce, suggesting that she lacked clarity of vision. Her behavior made legitimate the fears of whites that when some blacks came into positions of leadership they would make whites catch hell. I could only hope that she'd taken stock of her

6   Meaning, head nigger in charge.

obviously flawed judgment calls and learned from her mistakes. Time was soon to tell.

Meanwhile, I continued to be proud of my membership in the IAWP and looked forward to attending one of its conferences. However, every time I submitted an application to Barrett, the application was rejected. In contrast, another deputy who was not even a member of the IAWP was granted leave to attend more than one conference. During one of the sergeants' meetings, I decided to bring up the matter, calling attention to the fact my application again was rejected while another's always was accepted. The response was that I did not submit the correct request.

"What is the correct request?" I demanded in frustration. I never received an answer and continued to be tried and tested.

*

A rainbow also shone during 1996. During President Clinton's second term, the union president wanted a contingent of sheriffs and police officers to attend a rally in Macon, Georgia, which President Clinton was expected to attend. The union president called me at home and asked me to attend, speaking with me before he'd even consulted with the sheriff or secured her permission. After doing so, he called me again and informed me that Barrett said only five deputies could attend, to which he replied that I'd had already accepted one of the five slots. He didn't know if Barrett wanted to rescind her permission or what because he got the impression that she wasn't too pleased to hear that I was going or that who got to attend was out of her hands. At any rate, the union president further gave me the go-ahead to choose another deputy for one of the remaining slots while he chose two. Still later, I heard through the rumor mill that Barrett was surprised and taken aback to learn that I was contacted even before she was. How dearly I'd have loved to have been a fly on the wall of Barrett's office to witness her reaction!

At the televised and photo-blitzed rally, I witnessed that Atlanta Police sent approximately twenty-five officers. I wondered why we were given only five slots but dismissed it. The five of us received enough prominence, evident in two of us standing closest to the President to be photographed. I stood right next to him.

The following day, I was teased mercilessly and hailed as a celebrity because in the photograph President Clinton had his arm around my shoulder, to boot!

Maybe because of my somewhat celebrity status, I received a rare response from Barrett about my litany of grievances. I was dumbfounded! Barrett stated that she agreed with me regarding several points, in particular with the behavior that resulted in the shortage of staff. She also said due notice was being paid to my willingness to assist during those times of shortage. In fact, for a brief moment I had to pause and recollect what Barrett was referring to, and recalled that I'd first raised this issue the previous year, 1995. I'd written a memo pointing out that there never was enough help on the floors. Deputies were either attending a class or out sick. Additionally at meetings, I'd further argued that too many deputies were off on Sundays, and that days off were given based on favoritism, not seniority. I'd added that the conscientious deputies were doing their best; however, two deputies could not efficiently do the work intended for four. One area where this under-staffing was expressing itself negatively was in visitations. Inmates were beginning to be hostile and resentful that they could not see their visitors, or that their visits were cut short. It was only a matter of time before such deep anger exploded violently. I'd presented the written memos to this effect, all to no avail. Somewhat heartened by Barrett's response, I awaited the promised change.

It wasn't long before I and the other conscientious deputies realized that Barrett was merely applying a band-aid to an illness that required major surgery. How could the tumors of injustice by excised by a system that had its own metastasizing cancers and tumors? Indeed, Barrett's promises remained empty and hollow.

.

Chapter 8 — Fire Dancers

By 1997, the effects of an overcrowded jail and an absence of policy and procedures began to take its toll not only on me but the other diligent deputies who continued to feel the stress of working in such an environment and trying to keep morale high. We strove to maintain the policies; however, we were hard-pressed to do so. Hence, sometimes the inmates were taken from the floor without being handcuffed. In response to my memo regarding this matter, I received a response from the watch commander that I had the authority to correct any matter within my power. He pointed out that I had charge over other deputies and should I take the initiative to exercise it, I would be assisting him greatly. He promised that he would support my every decision and vouched that the sheriff would, also.

Then, I was completely blind-sided. My assigned deputies were being removed during the shift without my being informed. When a deputy was removed during a shift, the supervisor was supposed to be informed. I felt that this policy was being violated because I was a woman and being discriminated against and disrespected. I wrote a memo addressing this, which was ignored.

Because I was understaffed on the floor, when the inmates found a way to open all the doors by using chess pieces as makeshift keys, I began to feel fear for the first time. I feared not only for myself but for all the deputies who could be attacked on the floor without even going inside the zones. Also, it was drawn to our attention that items that could be shaped into weapons were missing. I sent off a memo to the captain, and copied it to the major, the chief, a second captain, and Sheriff Barrett. The safety of the deputies was paramount, and I was not going to risk their safety by adhering to protocol and bureaucracy or playing the politics-first game. To intensify my sense of urgency, I attached a drawing of the area made by another deputy where metal detectors for screening all inmates could be installed. I hoped the urgent tone of the memo would bring immediate action.

The response to this memo was a shakedown. All the inmates were handcuffed and placed in the day-room, having taken with them only their personal items, while their cells were thoroughly searched. The search resulted in multiple items being seized from cells that ought to have only single-item bed linens, towels, U/B shirts and pants, and sweat shirts. The search deputies also found parts of a cylinder block and a black rubber cord—items that could be used as deadly weapons. The areas from which these crude weapons-in-the-making were removed were located and marked for repair. The two inmates in whose cells these items were found were charged with illegal possession of a potential weapon. A potential disaster mercifully averted.

Meanwhile, another matter awaited addressing, one that compelled me to contact the IBPO. During a three-week reconstruction period of the parking lot, we learned at a meeting that there would be no lighting and the entire parking lot would be in darkness. I was beyond appalled. Such lack of lighting posed a threat to deputies and all visitors to the jail, official and civilian. Should anything happen to anyone, a major lawsuit would result. Thankfully, the idea of providing a generator with a light pole was already a feasible, non-costly answer. But that no one else saw the potential hazard this posed was mind-boggling. Were people simply sleepwalking on the job?

I began to feel like my mountain of memos written during 1998 and '99 would probably equal or surpass Mt. Aripo in height; still, I kept on submitting them. My next one addressed the inmates being served their liquids in heavy plastic cups. One didn't have to be Einstein or a rocket scientist to see that these cups could be easily broken and used to shank inmates and deputies alike. I wondered who expected the serving deputies to keep count of the cups when we didn't have enough deputies to keep count of the trays and other items. Common sense should have told everyone that heavy plastic cups were out of the question. So, I wrote a memo stating this. My patience was really wearing thin.

I now think most likely someone didn't like my tone because I stated quite bluntly that someone was lacking in common sense and being ludicrous or plainly oblivious to jail conditions to be so wasteful of the county's money by purchasing these hard, plastic cups. Another memo also raised questions regarding Human Resources' awareness of even the brooms being broken and used as weapons. Because our custodial staff was also small in number, the deputies themselves cleaned the floors. Some of them returned the brooms to locations inaccessible to the inmates while some deputies carelessly left them lying around. I had to call attention to such lackadaisical behavior, too.

Maybe someone finally felt that I'd written just about enough memos. It was after these last two that I felt like I'd been tossed into Nebuchadnezzar's fiery furnace, but there was no Jesus to show me how to sing songs whose sounds caused the blazes to retreat or turn the furnace into a deliciously warm sauna from which to emerge totally reinvigorated and still refusing to bow to any idol. It seemed that nothing I did met with approval, only with criticism. With every criticism, I filed a grievance that described how I felt that I was wronged. Many times, my grievance was ignored or dismissed as having been resolved at this level or unable to be resolved at another level. I myself sometimes paused and wondered whether some of the grievances were trivial or truly legitimate, but then stopped second-guessing myself. I was not responsible for creating an unhealthy, insecure working environment. Why should I allow my health and well-being to be jeopardized, only to regret it later? Wasn't I responsible to myself first and foremost? Thus, though my memos and grievances were inconvenient or maybe even a nuisance to someone, I felt compelled to keep on doing my best to help create a safe and wholesome working environment for everyone. I had started on a course and couldn't stop myself.

I was like a woman driven to right every wrong.

I ignored Grace's advice to back off. She was my number one confidante who listened without criticizing and offered advice only when I asked. She thought that I should feign blindness and deafness or else I would go mad, while also agreeing with me that the jail was filled with workers who should be behind bars themselves. She warned me to be careful not to ruffle any more feathers because people here were not as laid-back and easy-going as Trinidadians used to be. She pointed out that I too was not behaving like a Trini 'oman who lived and let lived.

She offered that I needed to go home, visit Las Quevas beach, enjoy some bake and shark, and stroll around Queen's Park Savannah while sipping on coconut water and munching on roasted corn. Grace has a way of painting an idyllic picture of home that made us both pause and question why we both left.

Still, I continued to ignore the small voice that said I couldn't fix the world and its problems, past or present. Instead, I persuaded myself that I could still leave it better for my having passed this way. God alone knows that I wasn't always this diligent about doing what was right. But I'd been attending bible studies and reading my bible daily. To me, the bible was written in black and white, literally and spiritually. You obeyed and were rewarded and blessed or disobeyed and were punished and lost. Simple and straightforward.

The bible story of Shadrach, Meshach, and Abednego really impressed me at one night's bible study. I imagined dancing inside a fire chamber whose heat killed its attendants who came into close proximity of it. I further imagined that I was dancing with Jesus in the fire chamber then felt ashamed of my thoughts because the bible doesn't say that Jesus danced. True, he'd attended a wedding and turned its water into wine but the story said nothing about dancing. But I loved to dance and hoped there'd be dancing in heaven. A God who made people who loved to dance must dance himself—or herself. I settled it with that understanding and didn't feel so guilty at the thought of my dancing within a fire chamber with Jesus.

While I battled for amelioration, I continued to complete all required coursework '98, and was especially proud when I completed the required coursework for Conversational, Intermediate, and Advanced Spanish for Public Safety Personnel. But a crowning moment came in

December when my fellow employees bestowed upon me the "Most Valuable Person" award that recognized my hard work and outstanding leadership. They additionally voted me "Deputy Sergeant of the Year." I could not but cry in appreciation of being so honored and esteemed among my co-workers. I must be doing something right, I reassured myself.

*

I'd maintained contact with Kim Loy Wong, my Trini steelband and carnival source of information. I could depend on his knowing what's what in the steelband world, his news being more efficient than any newspaper story. I also often asked if he'd heard about Ellie, my thoughts often returning to what I considered an open chapter of my life story.

Finally, one night I received a phone call from Kim; he'd heard that Ellie had settled in Morgantown, West Virginia, and was an artist-in-residence at West Virginia University, conducting annual steelband workshops. Even better, he had a phone number but warned me that Ellie was protected by a woman who screened his calls. However, knowing me he was confident that I could get past her.

I was pleased with the news that Ellie was doing well and debated whether to call him. One day, when I simply wanted to hear his voice, I picked up the phone and called the university instead of his home. He was on the road, so I left my name and number with one of the students instead. When he finally returned my call, our conversation began haltingly, "Hello."

"Hello."

"This is Maria."

"Who Maria?"

"Maria." I refused to volunteer any more, willing him to remember me.

Then he laughed, "Oh, my Maria." He'd not forgotten me. I laughed in return, happy in the knowledge of my womanhood, relieved that I mattered to someone who was not a girlfriend or family. And after all these years, it was like we'd spoken just yesterday and continuing an unfinished conversation, picking up where we'd left off. We talked for over an hour and caught up on each other's news. As we finished, he promised to stay in touch.

I hummed as I prepared for bed, "I am strong, I am invincible, I am woman!" I was back in Helen's choir and felt very good, confident once more that I could face whatever the world dished out and win.

*

The year 1999 began with the deputies' request for a salary increase, an issue that got some media attention. The argument we deputies presented was that our job was just as complex as any firefighter or policeman. In 1997, F.C.'s firefighters had received a pay raise equivalent to the county's police officers, while simultaneously the entry-level salary of sheriff and marshal personnel was increased to that of entry-level officers. The rest of the deputies now wanted salaries on parity with the firefighters and police officers. Why should we be the only ones to suffer for the county's financial deficit?

The deputies organized and held prayer sessions and continued to formally request the raises. We argued further that our job was just as complex, demanding, and dangerous as any police officers'. I , when being interviewed by Sandra Eckstein, staff writer for *The Atlanta Journal-Constitution*, asserted that protecting up to 350 jail inmates with two or three guards had its risks and challenges. Additionally, deputies were sometimes called upon to assist police in emergencies.

Charles Rambo, a union official, supported me and pointed out that the police and sheriff employees of the other counties—Clayton, Cobb, DeKalb, and Gwinnett—received comparable salaries. Why then should we of Fulton County be demoted to second-class status? Rambo's most compelling argument was the fact that some people who had worked for years were earning the same amount as the newly hired because starting salary levels were raised and other salary levels were not. As sympathetic as everyone was to the county's financial difficulties, it was unconscionable for anyone to expect morale to remain high in the face of such disparity.

Eventually, the deputies won and we received our salary increases.

*

The year 2000 brought its own spate of grievances. I filed against the following:

> the locks being changed without the deputies first being alerted.
>
> the unscheduled dinner time of some deputies.
>
> the sergeants who watched TV in the office.
>
> no drinking water in the towers.
>
> the constant shortage of staff.

Then, in June I received a memo from the training director that records indicated I failed to comply with the minimum firearms standards required of all certified department personnel, and that my firearm had been retained by the training section for the past three years. I was then reminded that I was required to return to the Firing Range for remedial training. I realized that all the medical waivers that certified my condition and exempted me from firearm training had fallen into some crack somewhere. I decided to attend to that matter immediately.

Once I cleared up the matter regarding my firearm training, I turned my attention to writing the lieutenant exam and passing it. Much to my consternation, when the results were released I was informed that I failed. When I requested to review my exam and score, I was denied. Meanwhile, others whom I thought couldn't possibly have passed learned that they passed and received promotions. It hurt me. I had been a sergeant since 1988 and deserved a promotion. Knowing full well that I was not a recipient of favoritism, I doubled my effort to pass the exam upon retaking it. I took the exam repeatedly, and each time I received a failing grade and was denied the right to review my exam and score.

At this time, Lynn was visiting. She had gone off her meds, quarreled with her boss, and stormed off her job. Finances almost depleted and no new job forthcoming, she asked me to use her old room. Without hesitation, I said yes and during these months was grateful for her companionship and not having to face an empty house.

Undaunted by the realization that I was being discriminated against due to my age and gender, I decided to take the matter to the EEOC and filed my complaints there. One of its supervisors informed me that my complaint was legitimate, advised me to proceed with it, and said that I should hear something shortly.

After two months and having heard nothing, one morning I phoned the office and spoke with another supervisor. This time, I was informed none too kindly that I didn't have a leg on which to stand. All my protests were cut off brusquely. I gritted my teeth in frustration. For the first time since I began fighting for what I believed, I got a glimpse of what drove some people to going ballistic and committing violence in the workplace as I felt myself slipping momentarily into that dark, evil recess of the mind.

I fantasized gleefully about going into the administrative wing of the Court House, the area in which Barrett's plush office was situated, and opening fire. I didn't want to kill anyone, however. Maybe I would just injure one or two, nothing fatal. Just inflict enough terror to shake things up a little and show them that I meant business. Heh, heh! I laughed grimly. I could really show them. I could go at a time when all the administrative officers and the sheriff were in a meeting and be an Annie Oakley. Then, I could plead temporary insanity and be committed to some mental asylum somewhere. I really didn't give a damn. I just wanted some satisfaction following months of frustration.

Then another image flashed across my mind. I saw the inmates housed and penned in the jail. So many of them reduced to shells of men. Just like *douens*. Men who looked and behaved like they had lost not only their way in the world but their very soul. Blank faces. Empty faces. Void of emotion. They rambled on in a language that only their deranged, diseased, disoriented mind or spirit or soul could follow. Heads thrown back and voices howling silently, hollowly to the wind. Black faces. White faces. Brown faces. Race and age didn't matter because when life was finished with chewing a soul into a shapeless, meaningless glob, it spat out the colorless phlegm into a stream that was ageless, weightless, colorless, and void of gender.

With all these grotesque, demonic images gyrating and taunting me to come on and join them after I'd taken satisfaction and bloodied my hands and ruined my worthless, good-for-nothing soul, I screamed. Then the scream became a low rumble that began somewhere inside and rose up and choked me in a guttural sound so that I almost fainted. Gasping and struggling to breathe, I reached out and gripped the kitchen table and eased myself into a chair, I thought. Instead, I missed and landed squarely on my buttocks, my head ricocheting off the wall with a couple of gentle thuds as I slumped to the floor. "God, no!" I gasped, "No! No! This can't be happening!"

As I remained on the floor, too weak to muster the strength to get up, from somewhere I heard another voice utter, "Lord, save me, again." Vaguely, I wondered whose voice that was because it didn't sound like mine. Sometime later, in my own voice, I said simply, "Lord, please save me, again, and again. For as many times as I need to be saved, I'm at your mercy only. So, please Lord, hear me now."

I waited for the Lord to reply. And still I waited, closing my eyes to block out the morning light that seemed to mock my utter distress. The sound of a mourning dove's cooing seemed fitting to my deep despair, and even so, I felt heartened by this sign of reality. Then, quietly and mysteriously, I felt a tug and that quiet voice I'd begun to call Mother reassure me that all will be well. And, I exhaled.

With a strong sense of what I must do, I arose, gathered my bag, checked my face in the mirror on the wall near the door, and went to my car.

At the office, I smiled at whomever greeted me, found the office telephone directory and returned home. There in the privacy of my family room, I called the Mental Health Department and set up an appointment for the next day to meet with the psychiatrist. Dr. Gregory Samples would have met with me that afternoon, if I wanted to, but I knew that I could survive the evening and night without resorting to any unredeemable behavior.

My eight visits with Dr. Samples helped return me to mental stability. He was completely the empathetic listener who understood the cause and nature of my harassment. With his experience and wisdom, he pointed out to me that as long as I was not a part of the office's inner circle I would be a victim, of sorts. I was omitted from activities that would provide information on what's what, without such I was bound to err, which then caused my errors to be examined under a microscope. That was just the way things worked. He was also not surprised that I was not invited to social events or the informal gatherings where tit-bits and goings-on were exchanged. Then, he offered how best I could cope, could rise toward overcoming my circumstance—with faith and prayer.

He made me promise to make Psalm 23, my favorite scripture, my daily and hourly prayer, and especially whenever I felt like I was losing control. Instead of losing control, I was to pause, take a deep breath and exhale slowly, and recite:

> *The Lord is my shepherd;*
> *I have all that I need.*
> *He lets me rest in green meadows;*
> *he leads me beside peaceful streams.*
> *He renews my strength.*
> *He guides me along right paths,*
> *bringing honor to his name.*
> *Even when I walk*
> *through the darkest valley,*
> *I will not be afraid,*
> *for you are close beside me.*
> *Your rod and your staff*
> *protect and comfort me.*
> *You prepare a feast for me*
> *in the presence of my enemies.*
> *You honor me by anointing my head with oil.*
> *My cup overflows with blessings.*
> *Surely your goodness and unfailing love will pursue me*
> *all the days of my life,*
> *and I will live in the house of the Lord*
> *forever.*[7]

Spiritually reinvigorated, with composure I could face a world I couldn't change and instead change the way in which I'd respond to repetitive flagrant abuses of privilege.

Taking his advice to heart, I began awaking every morning at half past five for private devotions that included bible reading followed by

---

7   Holy Bible, New Living Translation ®, copyright © 1996, 2004 by Tyndale Charitable Trust. Used by permission of Tyndale House Publishers. All rights reserved.

meditation then my exercise routine. Sometimes, I opened the bible randomly and read a chapter or two of that opened spot, believing that my randomness was linked to God giving me my daily reading. Then, I developed a more structured approach by trying to read it cover to cover. But I found the genealogies tedious and the laws of Deuteronomy to be dry so I gave up and settled on the wisdom of the Psalms, Proverbs, Ecclesiastes, and the Book of James.

The first chapter of James especially helped me to see that God was allowing me to go through this fiery-watery test to increase my faith and to make that faith in Him perfect. This I began after one bible study session that dealt with trials and persecution. Daring to think that I was being tried, I figured that maybe something good, beyond what I could see, was happening and took some comfort in that thought.

*

Spiritually and emotionally fortified, I faced with equanimity the apparent low to which the department had sunk. Sometimes, I wondered whether they were running a jail or a social club. There were the birthday parties or baby showers for which the Roll Call Room was closed to all but the celebrants. The first time I encountered one such celebration, I couldn't believe my eyes. I'd reported to the Roll Call Room and was told by a deputy to go to the dining room because a party was being held in the Roll Call Room. I wondered, "Does the sheriff know about this?!" Later, I realized that it was the members of her inner circle who were taking such liberties so it wouldn't matter whether she knew.

In fact, I dubbed an inner circle woman deputy the social events planner and executor because that was all she did. Rather than perform deputized duties, she baked, cooked, and fed the chosen few at their social events. What a life! It got even better for her, I observed. Whenever she happened to do a job-related task, it was merely to oversee the trustees. She also left the department two to three times, and each time she was rehired she returned to her cushiony, unofficial job as social events planner and executor. Officially, all deputies were supposed to have a radio with them. Not her. She never wore a radio, so no one could contact her if something was needed from the area in which she officially worked.

Without giving the impression of having singled her out, I reported to the watch commander that some deputies did not have their radios with them at all times. Of course, the watch commander did nothing about it. He probably knew exactly whom I was referring to and couldn't risk losing his baked goodies.

I made sure that I sent a copy of every complaint I lodged to the sheriff. I didn't want it to be said that she was unaware of what happened at the jail. Sometime later, rather than compliment me on my efficiency, as I dared to hope, my nemesis, Chief Briggs who was not yet fired, reprimanded me and asked me to stop sending copies to the sheriff. However, I continued to do as my conscience dictated, and copies of every complaint continued to flow like wild fire to the sheriff.

CHAPTER 9 — STARING INTO THE ABYSS

One night, I dreamt of being shoved down into a dark place that smelled of strong, foul chemicals, so odious that I felt myself fainting and heard the cacophony of horrible laughter interspersed with utterings in an incomprehensible language. But before I completely passed out, I awoke drenched in sweat. Heaving a deep sigh of relief that it was merely a nightmare, I arose and changed into a fresh nightie, changed the bed linens which were too damp and uncomfortable for me to fall asleep in, and sat on my bedside, bemused, wondering what the horrid dream meant. I gave up with the realization that I would just have to wait and see what the immediate future held for me. Sometimes, I dreamt quite clearly what was about to occur in my life, such dreams causing me to make life-saving decisions, even when I lived in Trinidad. Those dreams kept me from walking like a blind woman into many a ditch.

However, I found that I was now second-guessing myself, something I rarely, if ever, did. One reason I continue to be a Christian is that the New Testament makes sense to me. When I first read in the Second Book of Peter that the backslider was like a dog who returned to its vomit or a washed pig who returned to the mud, I didn't for one moment question the similes. Always, I'd lived with the attitude that what's done was done, for better or worse. So while there were some things about Trinidad that I'd rather never to remember, looking back and living in regret over what couldn't be changed didn't make sense. Now awake with all trace of sleep gone, I reflected upon my childhood.

*

East Indian neighborhoods were terrifying yet happy places in which to live. A typical neighborhood comprised of both Muslim and Hindu families. All East Indians were divided by marginal religious differences, I used to observe. The Trinidad dailies always featured stories of how one Hindu neighbor cut up his Muslim neighbor, or vice versa, because of something trivial, both men in a syzygetic dance, kept apart by their mutual animus.

For instance, one article reported how one neighbor sliced and diced another's face because the victim accidentally ran over an old hen who tried to fly out of the way of his new honking jeep but couldn't fly fast enough as old fowl and new jeep hurtled precariously along the bumpy road of the village.

The pock-marked road itself was a reflection of the village's—not the town's, the nation's, or the Caribbean's—development to date. The late 1950s had brought the insistent calls for independence from Great Britain. Why, if first the Middle East then India then the various African countries could break the British's stranglehold on them and cause the sun to begin to set on the British Empire, why not hasten the sunset by achieving a wave of independence of Caribbean countries? So, the sixties brought independence for the big four—Jamaica, Trinidad and Tobago, British Guiana renamed Guyana, then Barbados. With independence came the continued reliance on Great Britain and the United States who did not remove their presence from the countries. In fact, control continued and such was reflected in the roads.

Trinidad and Tobago should have the best paved roads in the world because of La Brea in Point Fortin, celebrated as the world's largest Pitch Lake, which Queen Elizabeth II visited to see for herself. This endless source of asphalt ought to have been used to surface and resurface every alley, lane, road, street, avenue, drive, boulevard, and highway throughout the country. Instead, only those that led to the homes of the colonial powers who resided in St. Clair, Bayshore, Glencoe, and Cascade were always smoothly paved and never reflected evidence of the Water and Sewage Authority's (WASA) latest project.

WASA was incessantly digging up roads to lay pipes or lines or whatever, and then proudly leaving the evidence of island progress in the dirt mounds, deep holes, and scattered bumps—of varying heights, depths, and widths—in its wake. An East Indian village in which no government official resided probably didn't even hold a place on the totem pole of priorities. Hence, its condition was left to be realized by anyone who chanced—rain or shine—to drive, dance, or hop along the road, the navigational feat being determined by the weather. Also, it was not uncommon for some roads to be paved to one point, unpaved for a few yards, and then paved again—the unpaved portion being owned by someone to whom the government refused to give their asking price for that little piece of land. The unpaved piece of road then made the unspoken statement to all and sundry, "Notice: Land owner resistant to government exploitation." As if the government cared!

*

In a typical East Indian village, on one side of the road were the icons that marked the Hindu homes from which blared loud Indian music that serenaded the entire village and beyond, and this before boom-boxes. Which said that some Indians figured out how to rig loudspeakers to radios to make music whose decibels penetrated the ears of a deaf man. These homes were adorned with red, yellow, and pink flags, some tattered and torn and some looking freshly washed, starched, and ironed. At the base of some flags were a shrine that included a bowl of boiled rice, some fruits, a photo or a figurine, garlands of yellow-red-and-white carnations, and some lit camphor or candles that paid homage to the household gods and goddesses or a deceased loved one. Sometimes in some neighborhoods, one would find that single house in front of which flew a white flag by a miscreant Hindu. He would explain his choice with one simple explanation. Foam from the Ganges River and foam from the Caroni River is still the same color. Likewise, a prayer that reached Krishna's ears had to come from a pure heart, one washed clean by Krishna's waters that flowed the same all over the earth. His prayer was one day to return to Krishna-land, an earnest prayer from a pure heart. 'Nuff said.

On the opposite side of the road were the Muslim homes that were unadorned by any religious symbols. In one village, to which many visitors flocked once upon a time, was the home of old Amīnah Khan who was not only the oldest person in the village but the one who was *the* most religious. Her front yard included a miniature mosque, which her son, The Right Honorable Minister of Cultural Affairs of Muhammad-Krishna Lane (a compromise, of sorts, you must see), the self-appointed arbitrator of peace, had built for her, Madame Khan. She insisted on being addressed as "Madame" when an important visitor came a-calling; otherwise, "Mistress Khan" did just fine. The villages must never forget that it was this beautiful mosque built by her son that brought visitors from near and far to admire it. The closest that the devoutly religious Muslim could get to a holy site that somewhat substituted for the Kaaba, the visit became a pseudo-pilgrimage. If one couldn't bring Muhammad to the mountain, then bring the mountain to Muhammad.

Regardless, all marveled that someone untrained in architectural skills could so perfectly replicate one of the wonders of the world, the great Taj Mahal, as it dared to guard Ganga Ma. Not that anyone of them had seen the original mosque to confirm that its Barataria replica was an exact one. Rather, the story went that someone from somewhere— who'd since evolved into a British aristocrat—came to visit old Amīnah Khan and had said that her mosque was the spit and image of the great Taj Mahal. Bless him and them all! Nor did anyone find questionable that Mother Ganges needed to be guarded by a human artifice. One day, She could rise up and completely inundate the great Taj Mahal. Should that happen, what would people say? What would people do? What would Muhammad come to signify to the peoples of the earth?

To return to the fate of the poor old hen, as reported in the dailies: according to the witnesses, Singh, the Hindu driver got out of the vehicle swearing at the old hen, calling the fowl such horrid names, and concluding that it was a creature that Krishna couldn't possibly have created. "Stupid-ass old fowls like t'at cud cum only frum Allah!"

And, what possessed him to invoke Allah's name in juxtaposition with "stupid," "ass," "old," and "fowl?"

Muhammad, the Muslim chicken-farmer, flew into a rage that equaled ten typhoons and twenty monsoons because Singh had "the bloody gumption to call Allah a 'stupid-ass, old fowl!' " And from nowhere, the witnesses continued, came one cutlass and one machete. And before anyone knew it, both men were a bloody mess requiring hospitalization and receiving one hundred and one stitches each. If the dailies had followed their discharge and return to their village to recuperate, they would have reported that both men swore the vengeance of his respective god to strike his enemy dead.

That incident was mild in contrast to others that didn't make the dailies' headlines. Those regarding violence against wives, whether East Indian or African, or interracial. Too many women with broken bones that paled in comparison to their broken spirits. Too many daughters who continued in the cycle of violence. Any night, a woman could be heard bawling out, "Murder! Help me! He go kill meh tonight! Murder! Help!" And in response, "Shet yuh bleedy mout'! If yuh know w'at good feh yuh! Shet up! Take that! And that! And that!" with what sounded like loud thuds. The following day, the village would be abuzz with how he stomped and kicked his wife into unconsciousness, and now it looked like she was going to remain so. Why? Because he came home and didn't like what he found. Or, because she asked him for more money for the market. Or, simply because she was there for him to take out his frustrations on.

If he went too far in the beating and she died, which happened much too often, the bereaved husband would miraculously become the holiest Muslim who prayed more than five times a day, the most devout Hindu who would die for Krishna, or the Christian who surpassed Christ's compassion and humility, giving the woman the most lavish funeral with originally composed dirges that awed mourners and beckoned them to follow the paid women mourners to ululate all the way to the cemetery. As though the fact that he'd killed her could be compensated by his display of repentance and generosity, when posthumous repentance and generosity merely mounted to a hill of beans.

Men and religion. The religions of men, their tools of oppression. Why, when, and how did the mothers surrender their power to men so men could destroy and kill sometimes with impunity? In the name of what religion did such terror for women first begin to stalk the earth? This ubiquitous tool that causes much of the world's miseries and sufferings must have been forged in hearts and minds that saw themselves as final authorities, as laws unto themselves. How do they differ from Homer's Cyclops who was protected by his father, Poseidon? Whose goddess's power was stripped so that she could no longer protect women? But even worse, what blinded women in power so much that they forged alliances with evil men and acted oppressively toward women, their own kind? When would it end?

*

So much about life continued to be baffling to me. Like Barrett. She was behaving like a *souciyante*,[8] sucking the life from her sisters with whom she ought to have formed solidarity toward easing and relieving our subjugation. Was that too much to expect? I wondered what hell-pit spawned Barrett and sent her into this existence to make life so miserable for so many in her charge. Were they aware of what they'd unleashed when they voted her sheriff? Sometimes, I wondered whether she rigged the election to grab the reins of power that she then so ineptly managed. When one enters into a position and one's integrity already is being viewed through the prism of compromise, respect then must be earned and kept. Otherwise, a stumble would not be regarded as evidence of human frailty but as proof positive of corruption. A slip may not be overlooked as a momentary lapse in judgment but rather perceived as a sign of untrustworthiness. Who then with a sane mind could look at Barrett and see anything good in her leadership? Sometimes, I wondered whether I was being too harsh or judgmental. Then an incident occurred to confirm that my intuition continued to be right.

From the first time I saw her, a deep sense of foreboding began to haunt me. Now, it seemed like a thick, heavy blanket of darkness

---

8   A female vampire.

was thrown over my head threatening to suffocate me. My bedroom suddenly felt very hot at three o'clock the pre-dawn hour. I went downstairs to the TV room, the coolest room in the house. I suddenly didn't want to be in my bedroom alone but I didn't want to watch TV either, I realized while sitting there.

I stared at the blank screen for an indeterminate length of time.

I returned upstairs to the bedroom and opened a window to let in some fresh air and to let out whatever was trying to stifle me. Sitting down again on the side of the bed, I stared at the digital clock on the end table and thought, "The blinking colon could be hypnotic, if I allowed it to mesmerize me." I began counting each blink, "One, two, three," and began imagining being sleepy when I got to sixty. Then, the sudden hum of the refrigerator's motor resuming its cycle startled me. Calming down, I listened to it to see if that would have a somniferous effect, then swung my legs up onto the bed and laid down. Closing my eyes, I listened to the refrigerator's hum and it seemed like a few moments later that the alarm awoke me from a fitful sleep.

While I should have been sluggish and sleepy, I felt surprisingly alert and energetic. I completed my morning rituals mechanically while I continued to reflect upon the ways in which women have suffered in this world and the courage with which they've resisted becoming partners in their oppression, winning some battles and losing some:

The Mirabal sisters, *tres mariposas hermosas*, who for the revolution sacrificed their lives toward the fall of Trujillo, the violence they experienced birthing the "International Day for the Elimination of Violence against Women."

Patrice Gaines, who in her darkest hour laughed at Gabriel, refusing to be broken in will or spirit to become one of his prostitutes.

Ayaan Hirsi Ali, who has defied the threat of fatwa to protest misogyny that was protected by religion to say enough is enough.

The return of slavery in the form of the international trafficking of girls and young women into prostitution and the many who've escaped to call attention to this dehumanizing treatment.

The return of slavery in the form of *sans papiers*, the stripping of the identity or citizenship of women from third world countries in first world countries, a status that forces them to be at the complete mercy of their abusive mistresses.

Those whose identity will forever remain enshrouded in the statistics of a United Nations Development Fund for Women (UNIFEM) report:

Somewhere in America a woman is battered, usually by her intimate partner, every fifteen seconds (United Nations Study on The World's Women, 2000).

A woman is raped every twenty-three seconds in South Africa (Rape Crisis Cape Town, 1998).

Every minute in the United Kingdom, police receive a call from the public for assistance for domestic violence. Eighty-one percent of these are female victims attacked by male perpetrators (Economic and Social Research Council's Programme on Violence, Royal Holloway, September 28, 2000).

Forty-seven percent of women in Bangladesh have been physically abused in their lifetime by an intimate partner (WHO, Database on Violence against Women, 2000).

*

Upon arriving at work, the meaning of my dream and insomnia was clear. I was reassigned to Supply, a position whose office was in the basement in a room adjacent to where the cleaning chemicals were kept. Clearly not an office or intended for office use, it was a storage room converted into a makeshift office. The hurt that I felt due to this new attempt to humiliate me was unbearable. I couldn't even cry in despair. I simply stood there, head bowed, as a new wave of depression descended. Determined, however, not to allow this new assignment to get the better of me, I managed to complete a month in that environment.

Psalm 23 continued to be my mantra.

I may have remained there longer except that I began to suffer the effects of an allergic reaction to the chemical fumes. By mid-morning one day, I marched upstairs and announced that I had an emergency doctor's appointment, left the office, and drove to the doctor's hoping that he would see me.

After describing my symptoms—headaches, nausea, pain in my arms and legs, he sent me to a Rheumatoid Specialist. The specialist diagnosed the cause of my discomforts as the chemicals I was inhaling, having arrived at this conclusion after several blood tests and an MRI. She prescribed for me six weeks of sick leave.

Upon returning to work, I requested of my supervisor, Lt. Beavers, to be moved from Supply, since I was diagnosed as having suffered an allergic reaction to the chemical fumes. He responded that chemicals were all over the jail. I pointed out, however, that in the basement there were no windows, no ventilation. Seeing that he was adamant, before going to the captain, I decided to take some photos of the area used for storing the chemical drums, brooms, and mops and present them as proof while apprising him of my condition and request. With the evidence to support my request, the captain immediately assigned me to a different location. Later, I learned that the large drums were removed from Supply.

The after-effects of having been exposed to the chemical fumes required me to remain on medication for over six months and to be absent from work without pay, since I'd depleted all my paid sick leave. Later, while discussing this with my union representative, I was informed that I ought to have received Workers Compensation, since my illness was caused by the unhealthy environment to which I was subjected.

Consequently, I decided to hire a lawyer to handle my case, the hope of which was to be paid for my sick leave. It was then I discovered the lengths to which my opposition willingly chose to go in order to deny me my rights and to prevent me from getting paid. Both the chief and my own supervisor conspired against me. I had secured as a witness Corporal Bryan Turner who had written a letter attesting that while working in Supply, he also had been affected by the chemicals left uncovered in barrels. His memo specifically stated he worked the 3-11 shift for two years and experienced headaches from inhaling the fumes emitted from the ammonia-based floor stripper, floor sealer, floor wax, ammonia-based glass cleaner, bleach, and disinfectant. Consequently, he was subpoenaed to appear on my behalf. The chief, however, never gave Turner the subpoena, so he never knew when he was to appear at Court.

Meanwhile, the County hired its own doctor who testified that he was sure my doctor had misdiagnosed my condition. Additionally, both Chief Briggs and my supervisor, Lt. Beavers, testified against me, making it appear as though I simply found an illness lurking behind the slightest cough and sneeze. Briggs, the first to testify, volunteered without solicitation that I also complained about everything and everyone, including workers who smoked, having to walk to my job, and carrying a gun. In fact, he could only conclude that I was unhappy with my job and some sort of hypochondriac. My lawyer objected that mine was not a criminal case nor was his client's character on trial, and that the defense should stick to the facts related to the case. The judge sustained the objection and ordered the comments, which were not a part of the deposition, to be stricken from the records. I could plainly see that Briggs's moment of planned triumph was struck down, and he was not happy about that. When called to testify, Beavers swore under oath that he never received any notice of my illness. Consequently, I lost my case.

Fate's untimely hand intervened, and a couple of months later while going through my Human Resources files, I found all the documents I needed to negate Beavers's testimony. There before my eyes were the doctor's notes that I had submitted to him, the call-in sick slips that he'd signed, and the Turner subpoena. I circumspectly xeroxed them all and took them to my attorney who regretted that I hadn't found them earlier. He said that we had sufficient grounds for appeal; however, I decided to allow the matter to drop. I recognized that my opposition stuck together so tightly that not even a whisper of a wind could pass between them. I knew that they would simply find another water-proof basket into which to place my baby case and send it sailing down the Savannah River. I could just see them waving bye-bye to the truth, with diabolically triumphant sneers on their faces.

As I departed from my attorney's office that morning, I lifted my face to the sun and prayed, "See, Lord, in the face of the evidence that I've been wronged, I will not have the satisfaction of wining this case. In fact, Lord, I'm letting it go. But I know, Lord, that I've already won it. How? That's what you're working out. What you've already worked out on my behalf.

"Lord, it hurts like hell that I'm not getting immediate satisfaction, that I won't get the money that I've worked for and deserve. And you know how much that hurts because I'm not rich, and I'm not looking to become rich. Only for what is fair. What I've worked so hard for all these years.

"But Lord, the bigger injustice is the extent to which my enemies have conspired against me. It's now I think that I understand what David meant when he wrote, 'Contend, O Lord, with those who contend with me; fight against those who fight against me.... Say to my soul, 'I am your salvation.' Because, yes, Lord, *You* are *my* salvation through all of this. And, one day I will prevail. I will be the conqueror.

"Until then, may I live to see all my enemies fall by the wayside, just as David saw his enemies fall. And when they fall—for fall they surely must because Your principle of Truth and Righteousness cannot be violated—I will dance like David danced, and sing like David sang, even now as I pray as David prayed. Amen."

As if to test my faith, the following weeks were replete of hostility and resentment toward me. My coworkers turned up the heat to what felt like two hundred degrees. All man jack banded together against me to make my life a living hell, it seemed. For instance, when I complained to higher ranking officers, they all sympathetically admitted to knowing that I was being unfairly harassed but claimed that there was nothing really that could be done about it. I could either deal with it or quit. Never one to quit, I resorted to more therapy and prayer.

CHAPTER 10 — UNEXPECTED FRIENDSHIPS

Momentary relief came just when I thought I would have to quit and save my life. My next assignment was in Reception. Little did I know that I was beginning to be the ball in a ping pong game: or was it a cat-and-mouse one? Whichever game it was, I lacked the agency, though not the will, to effect a turn toward my winning. Because after a few weeks in Reception, the chief ordered my supervisor to move me, his reason being there was no need for a sergeant in Reception. But I knew better.

In Reception, as previously mentioned, I could see the front area of the jail, could observe the behavior of all the employees. In a matter of days, I witnessed how the deputies of the inner circle abused their privilege. Apparently, some of them had part-time jobs elsewhere and managed their time accordingly. They clocked in at the jail, hung around for a few minutes, left, then later returned to clock out as if they'd spent the entire day at the jail. Others took two-hour dinners, when officially dinner was afforded only half-an-hour.

The most egregious offence related to the Reception area door, which was supposed to remain closed. Only personnel assigned to that area were permitted. Before I supervised the area, deputies from other parts of the jail habitually took a shortcut through the door. Even civilians who worked at the jail were treated with laxity, when this was supposed be to a secure area.

Once I began to insist on abiding by policy, everyone became offended, in particular those who'd become accustomed to the laxed policy. Visitors who were supposed to be thoroughly searched were indignant at being subjected to a thorough search. The most insulted were church musicians who'd sailed by with their carrying-case not being thoroughly inspected, if at all. Now searched, they felt that instrument cases though ideal containers in which to smuggle in weapons couldn't possibly apply to them because they were church-people. By implication, they were supposed to be treated as above the law. They could not see how their arrogance contradicted the teaching that Christians were also required to humbly and in all ways abide by the law. Christians were supposed to be exemplary. When I brought to the chief's attention this last breach of policy, he countered that the searches were conducted on the floors of the housed inmates. I, however, knew that was a blatant lie. I'd worked the floors and no one ever searched the church musicians. Period.

*

My next assignment was The Property Room. There, I was convinced that maybe this was not just man's doing but God's, too. I was surely and sorely being punished for all my sins, even though I didn't kill a priest, as they said in Trinidad. Nonetheless, I prayed asking, "God, what Father or priest have I killed? What sin did I commit that deserves such punishment, one followed by another? You said in Your Word that You wouldn't give me more than I can bear. How am I supposed to bear this?"

The Property Room was where all the inmates' unlaundered articles of clothing were stored in bins for weeks, untouched. This room, similar to Supply, also had no ventilation or windows, so the rank odor was overpoweringly nauseating and eye-tearing. I reeled back instinctively upon first entering and being blanketed suffocatingly by the strong sulphuric stench. Covering both my nostrils and mouth, I gazed in utter dismay at the sight and retreated backwards until I was outside, holding back a wave of nausea that threatened to spill out. If the smell of vomit were added to sulphur, no one would have been able to enter the area for weeks. When outside and refreshed by deep gulps of fresh air, my rationale returned. Surely, I'd just glimpsed at and smelled hell. Surely, I must have seen hell's demons dancing in glee around and on top of each barrel. Surely, I must be losing my mind. I'd heard other deputies complain but accept their assignment to Property, but I'd lacked the imagination to think it was this bad! Surely, I'd been assigned to Property to finally gag me. Or break my will. Not in the least.

I immediately filed a complaint, and a Workers' Compensation inspector was dispatched to investigate the condition. He was also a reserve deputy who occasionally volunteered at the jail for a few hours a week. Whoever got to him first must have persuaded him to slant his report which read:

> *After receiving a complaint from Sergeant Maria Pereira, which alleged that the inmates' Property Room lacks ventilation, I investigated this complaint immediately and found that there is a sufficient amount of air-flow in the area. In fact, it is so cool that some deputies who have served in this area have had to wear their jackets. There is a smell, but the smell is not so strong that it could cause a person to get sick.*

After receiving a copy of the Memorandum Report, I took it to the chief and pointed out that the report could not possibly be truthful, honest, or professional. First, the investigating deputy was not a doctor and in no position to determine what can cause a person's illness. Second, why has he never volunteered to work in Property, if conditions were so bearable? In fact, why has he always worked in areas farthest from Property?

I became even angrier while speaking with the chief and observing his manner. He avoided my eyes, pretending to be busy with something on his desk. So, though I was a Christian and had vowed to leave the strong language of my old self in the past, I found myself cursing and swearing angrily. It was then he looked up in alarm and I paused to catch my breath. Watching his reaction, I thought, "So this is the only language men like you understand. You provoke people to deep anger then feel justified in saying that we immigrants are discontented and hard to please."

Utterly disgusted at myself for allowing them all finally to get under my skin, of going back on my word, of being on the verge of tears, I stormed out of his office but not before I reasserted my dignity and reclaimed my integrity.

Taking a deep breath, I began, "Now that I have your undivided attention, Chief, let me continue by saying that I finally get the extent to which you hate me. I must be a real slow learner, but I think I get it. And that part of your hatred is to crush me. But take a good look at me, this woman, this East Indian woman who done take some hard knocks in life. So, hear me good when I say, in no uncertain terms, that I am aware that I may be at the losing end of the stick here because I can't fight all of you in power. All of you have conspired against me to make me look like a trouble-maker, someone who is just discontented, an immigrant who's come from some third-world country and having life good for the first time. Oh, yes; I've heard the snickers and whispers behind my back.

"You all can think what you like and say what you like. That's your prerogative. But know mine, at the same time. I'm a woman who's old enough not to play games either on or off the job because I take my work and the honor it brings very serious.

"I also have my integrity to maintain, sir. It has always been my nature to speak up and stand up for what is right. People have not liked this about me, sir, and I don't apologize for this. I have and will continue to bring to attention conditions and treatment that are unfair and wrong, sir. If for that I am made to look like a fool, then that is not my problem. I'm aware that it has made my working here quite uncomfortable for many, including myself. But know this, at the end of the night, I leave here with a clear conscience. I sleep well at night with a mind at ease with itself.

"People don't believe my age or my occupation when I so inform them, sir. But that is because I live so that when I face my Maker, I will hear, 'Well done.' It's the higher authority I answer to.

"So, I've filed complaints instead of merely grumbling like everyone else who's done little or nothing to change things around here that needed to change. I've tried to get support and think I've gained it;

however, the other deputies so often have backed out at the last moment and left me hanging out to dry. One such time was when the Captain decided to change assignments at the last moment. All the sergeants decided to file a grievance. We decided, however, that before filing we'd meet with the major. Then, on the day of the meeting, I was the only one who showed up for the meeting. He said that he couldn't take the matter any further because I was the only one complaining. It was from then on I decided that I could rely only on myself, sir. I also learned that administration could violate any policy or procedure because they knew they could get away with it, that no one would complain. No one but me."

Seeing that I finally had his undivided attention, I felt my confidence increase. I continued with even more confidence in my voice, which was a little shaky before, "And, for that, I've been marked a trouble-maker. Trouble-maker, my foot! They talk to me like I'm some imbecile, trying to make *sut* of me because I have an accent. And this whole thing about black people with an accent being retards, isn't that evidence of your own racist bias? And if you asked me, racist hypocrisy, too, because I don't see you treating white people with accents, especially a British one, as imbeciles.

"Instead, all of you call me an ungrateful immigrant and say I should go back to where I came from. You all call me black, Hispanic, Indian, whatever you feel, and have never taken the time to find out what or who I am. So, I've suffered all forms of discrimination from all of you: age, race, gender, and culture. Four strikes against me to teach me to know my place in this U.S. society.

"But tell me, Chief, when did the U.S. stop being an immigrant country? When did the American Dream stop being the goal that all man jack striving for? When did 'pulling yourself up by your bootstraps' come to apply to only a chosen few to make something of themselves?

"So, Chief, if you or anyone else can answer me these questions so that I could understand that America never was the land of immigrants and never will have a place for people like me, then I'll quit. Otherwise, if you and the department want to get rid of me, you'll have to fire me. Regardless of how much pressure you all put on me, I will *not* quit. And now that *you* know exactly where *I* stand, all I finally want to say is what we say in Trinidad, 'Yuh cud take that, put it in yuh pipe, an' smoke it.' "

Without awaiting his response, but after seeing a flicker of something—I'd like to think a begrudging admiration—in his dark brown eyes, I walked out of his office, feeling good that I'd regained my composure and not given way to blubbering and tears.

That night, I called Grace. She didn't want to hear the details over the phone and came directly over. Exhausted, I recounted all the details with much satisfaction. She cried, laughed, and hugged me. But she so wished that things were going better. She made me a cup of green tea, made sure that I finished it before leaving. I crawled into bed and immediately fell into a deep, dreamless sleep.

I slept like a baby from then on. No more nightmares or sweats to awake me.

*

It was of no surprise that the next week I was reassigned to the medical unit. On my first day, I had to clean up its untidiness, which I did with the help of some inmate trustees with whom I continued to maintain a relationship of mutual respect. That Christmas, I received some heart-warming, hand-made cards from a few of them.

Merry Christmas Sgt. Pereira

CERTIFICATE
OF

APPRECIATION

Sgt. M. PEREIRA, IS
granted this Certificate by the Inmate's
IN, 7N200. We the Inmates of 7N200, really do APPRECIATE
your help around here, even when your not here, your presence
IS still felt near, 'cause', were so used to you coming IN
here.
We'll always have respect for you, not just "because", your a
female Sgt., "But", because you are you.

You look out for us, whenever we need INformation, OR RICE st.
things, you comes IN with a smile, that Spead's a
Mile long.

Jingle Bell, Merry Christmas and a Happy
New year, have fun, enjoy yourself, "but', be
Careful, 'cause', this IS the Best Time of year.

This 22 DAY of Dec. 98.

7N200
Representatives

211 Rick Wilkey
203 Donald Smith
208 Quintus Smith
207 James Jones
214 _____

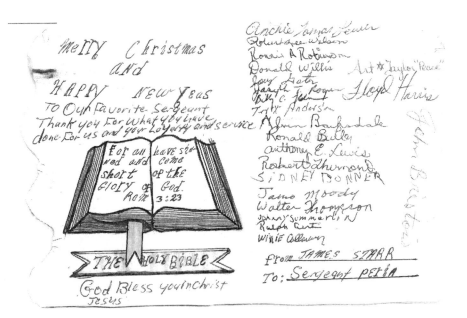

MerrY Christmas
aNd

HAPPY NEW YEAS
TO Our Favorite Sergeant
Thank you For What you have
done for us and your Loyalty and service

For all have sin
ned and come
short of the
GloRY of God.
Rom 3:23

THE WHOLE BIBLE

God Bless you in Christ
Jesus

Archie Jamas Lewis
Robert Lee Wilson
Ronnie A Robinson
Donald Willis   Art * Taylor "Peace"
Gary Gator
Jacryph J Rogers   Floyd Harris
Billy C. Jent
Tony Anderson
Alvin Barksdale
Ronald Bulley
anthony E. Lewis
Robert Thurmond
SIDNEY DONNER
Jame Moody
Walter Thompson
Johnny summerlin N
Ralph Cunt
WiniE Calloway

From JAMES STARR
TO: Sergeant PETER

To the Best
Sergeant
I Know

Bless You And Love
Always

Gift of Love ...

I wish I could send a new car
a new house, or a dimond ring.
But all I can give is my love
and hope that some joy it brings.
It's not tied with pretty ribbon
or a package tied with string.
It's just a gift that comes from
my heart that lasts through
  Winter and Spring
    Merry Christmas
      With Love Always

          Marvin Robinson

*

Word must have circulated that my presence was doing some good because I learned that a male sergeant, one belonging to the inner circle, wanted to work in Medical. Once more I was reassigned to the female cell block where male deputies were not allowed to work. Here, a fresh set of problems arose among those who sought to violate policy.

Knowing full well that male deputies weren't allowed on the floor, some of them frequented the floor. One of them was caught having sex with a female inmate and reassigned to the Court House, not fired. Hence, whenever I was on duty, I asked them to leave. My stringent adherence to the policy didn't bode well, so I was reassigned. The ping pong ball continued to bounce. The rolling stone gathered no moss.

My next assignment was to the Seventh Floor, which housed maximum security inmates. Policy and Procedure, if followed, mandated that four deputies and one sergeant were supposed to be on the floor at all times. All the floors were always understaffed because most of the deputies being hired were young females, and as soon as they were assigned to the Seventh Floor they became pregnant and had to be reassigned. Because I didn't fall into that pattern, I aimed to remain on Seventh and out of the chief's and everyone else's way for a while. I didn't mind. My only complaint was that sometimes the Seventh Floor had only two deputies and me. Sometimes, we'd be reduced to only me and one deputy. I filed several related complaints and always received some so-called valid excuse.

However, the situation was grave. The inmates often unlocked their cell doors, which was a real security breach. Mostly, these breaches occurred when I wasn't on duty. The inmates respected me for doing my job and cooperated with me. Additionally, I treated them firmly but fairly, a manner that Sgt. Heidi Schaefer and I had down pat.

Heidi was one of the few friends I could count on to back me up against the chief. She was white and out of the chief's lecherous range, but was sometimes subjected to occasional inappropriate comments because she and I supervised according to Policy and Procedures and ran our section by the book. She also was not hesitant to speak her mind, and I smiled with grim satisfaction whenever she told off anyone who harassed her. She had the wind of rightness in her back. Going to work was much easier knowing that Heidi and I walked in lockstep regarding Policy and Procedure.

Another reliable friend was Captain Cynthia-Dum-Zachery.

Cynthia was the only high ranking female officer who responded positively to my complaints. She was in charge of the Laundry and Commissary, and one of her jobs was to make sure the jail was kept clean. She insisted on the daily mopping of the floors, cleaning of the bathrooms, toilets, and elsewhere. Several times when the area I was assigned to was not cleaned properly, I called her. Immediately, she made sure herself that everything was in tip-top condition. She was not only hard-working and fastidious, she also kept her subordinates in line, all the while making sure that everyone respected her not only because she was a Captain but also because she was a woman.

*

Slowly, I grew to respect some of the inmates more than I did some of my coworkers, particularly those who had part-time jobs elsewhere. These deputies slept when they came up on the floors instead of doing their job and were not reprimanded because they were buddies with watch commanders who turned a blind eye when they left to go to their part-time jobs. They sometimes made me think that more offenders of society needed to be behind bars.

CHAPTER 11 — STANDING STILL

Meanwhile, I continued to pursue my goal to rise to the highest rank possible. I was still determined to be promoted to the next level of lieutenant. Once more, I took the required test and again was not given my test score. Determined not to be deterred, I took the test again, and then again. Still, my scores were withheld.

Recognizing that the reasons were invalid, once more I began the process of filing grievances, of which nothing came. Instead, to add insult to injury, several of the deputies whom I trained received promotions. Finally wearied down, I gave up taking the test and swallowed my deep disappointment, not recognizing that the persistent pain I'd developed in my right shoulder was related to my swallowed pain. A pain that made it impossible for me to qualify at the gun range. Since I was confined to the jail and did not have to wear a weapon, I did not qualify with my weapon for about five years. I took only a forty-hour class that was required by Post; instead of qualifying with a weapon, I took another class. I also again turned in a doctor's note, as I'd done in previous years, that stated the reason for my not going to the gun range.

Very reluctantly, I began to face some truths. One, I was finally tired of filing complaints and grievances to no avail. Two, it would be in my best interest to simply take the lieutenant-level test one more time and then retire so I could at least get more money as a retired lieutenant. I didn't imagine that someone had decided that regardless of how I actually performed on the test, I would always receive a failing grade. Lurking somewhere in my consciousness, I believed that they would eventually acknowledge that I'd pass. A truly vain belief. I again saw deputies who had minimal knowledge of the test material succeed, while I with superior knowledge failed.

Incidentally, on the very day that the letter arrived announcing that I'd failed once more, I also received a letter from the sheriff informing me that I did not qualify with my weapon and was given a certain length of time to respond to the letter or be terminated. I felt that familiar sick feeling in the pit of my stomach. These people would stop at nothing in their efforts to utterly destroy me, I thought as I sat down in despair at my desk. Then I collected myself, took a deep breath, and phoned my union representative. After discussing briefly with him the latest development, he offered to make an appointment for me to see the sheriff. But this time, a feeling of defeat pervaded my entire being and I asked him not to. Why did I have to fight and defend my every action? Why was I being so persecuted at every turn? What had I done wrong? What was I doing wrong?

I recalled reading in the New Testament that Jesus said his servants would not be treated better than their Master. One friend at church in whom I'd confided made the observation that I was being harassed by Satan, the enemy of every Christian, who attacked the newly saved or old and seasoned alike. God was allowing the testing so that I'd come out shining like pure gold. I groaned. If this was my testing by fire to remove all the dross and sludge from my heart and mind, a purification process, then Good Lord, it hurts like hell. Did it have to be so painful?

In resignation, I decided not to fight any more. I'd do nothing and await their next move.

When I was called to meet with Barrett at the end of November, I attended the meeting already having decided to accept whatever was offered, and display all the dignity and Christ-like behavior I could muster, and allow the Spirit to shine through me.

At the meeting, I was strangely calm. A peace settled over me that I knew came from the Source of life and love. I looked at Sheriff Barrett, measured somewhat distractedly and dispassionately her uneasiness, and noted her failure to look me squarely in the face as she said mechanically, as though she'd rehearsed every word, what she had to say. I also registered that her crony, Stanley Greene, was seated beside her and shaking his head and muttering in agreement with everything she said. Barrett's voice sounded tinny as she recited, "Sergeant Pereira, I have a letter for you. Please take your time and read it carefully. Afterward, I'll be happy to answer any questions you may have."

Gingerly, I reached over and took the letter from Barrett. I began to read the letter that was titled, "Termination from employment with Fulton County Georgia." My mouth turned dry and my stomach lurched because I really didn't anticipate this blow. It couldn't be real, their ultimate plan to gag me, once and for all. I read on and noted the grounds for my dismissal were: one, my failure to qualify at the firearm test for three consecutive years; and two, for not having provided a reasonable excuse for my failure to meet the requirement. I knew that they didn't have to go hunting for this evidence but that they must have buried my medical records. I had my copies and could still get my doctor to issue whatever was necessary to vindicate me. I also noted that a date—less than a week away—was scheduled for me to return and discuss the matter.

In the following days, I learned that my only option was to accept a demotion from Deputy Sheriff Sergeant to Detention Officer II. Hence, I returned to the meeting with my letter of acceptance of my demotion, and that I was aware that my salary would not be affected. The only thing I needed to remind Barrett of was that I did not have any Detention Officer uniforms. Barrett advised me to see the new chief jailer about that matter, which I did; however, I never received my uniforms.

On January 30, 2001, I received an official letter notifying me of my voluntary demotion, which entailed the cessation of duties related to Deputy Sheriff Sergeant. It was like a stab in the heart.

Even harder was my having to deal with the deputies at the demoted rank. Many of them were much younger than I and had egos that were so large they were engulfed and drowning in them. Nevertheless, they knew that I was excellent at the job and some of them grudgingly afforded me all due respect. I had no problems with the few who always maintained a high level of professionalism and made the environment bearable.

*

In April, I was ordered to report to duty wearing my Detention Officer uniform because I'd had ample time to acquire them. I replied that due to the inefficiency of the department, the order was still being processed and when I received them, I'd be happy to wear one. Until then, I would be grateful not to be harassed about a matter over which I had no control. I was calling my shots and that included, "Bug off and leave me alone. There's nothing more you can do to me now."

Sometime later, I learned from a coworker that one of the detention officers working in the court was promoted to DO III, a position that was never posted so no one could have applied for it. I half-heartedly filed another grievance which got no response, as I expected. Obviously, the Grievance Board was under Barrett's thumb. It ruled in favor of whatever she said, whether the aggrieved party was right or wrong. Sometime later, yet another deputy who failed the gun range was promoted to DO III. This time, I took my complaint to the union who filed for an open record and discovered that several deputies did not qualify at the range; however, they kept their rank. It was then the sheriff was forced to take action and demote a few deputies. She dared not risk another lawsuit.

*

I continued to execute my duties according to my conscience. I received another memo calling attention to the fact that I was still out of uniform. However, I'd covered my back by that time. I'd made a genuine goodwill effort to acquire at least one set of uniforms but was unsuccessful. I'd even tried to buy a set from a sanctioned vendor but was also unsuccessful. It was not my fault that I'd been demoted when uniforms were not being allotted. In response to finally addressing the matter, I pointed this out to the Captain, who agreed with me and allowed the matter to go to the chief. The only hope was that eventually at least one set of uniforms would be available and I'd be left in peace.

If they thought my demotion would silence me, they had another thing coming. I remained silent until May the following year when the paint fumes of Building 2-F caused me and two other employees—one a female sergeant and the other a male lieutenant—to be dizzy and nauseous. In fact, it was the male lieutenant who immediately protested against the hazardous working conditions. The strong fumes also threatened the health of the inmates. The lieutenant said he was going to call about the problem and that they should all leave before they passed out. I went home and later received a call from another sergeant inquiring about my well-being and informing me that the other sergeant had been taken to the hospital because she almost fainted due to the fumes. I enjoyed an extended sick leave and filed the related grievance.

Upon my return, I resumed my role of watch-woman keeping things in line. Once, one of the female deputies began to make a spectacle of herself. Whenever she worked the floors, every time she had to make a security round, she applied extra make-up and heavy perfume. As her supervisor, I took her aside one day and advised her to tone it down because the inmates and deputies were talking about her, saying that she was enticing the inmates. She completely ignored my advice.

On a day when I was off the floor performing another chore, an emergency call sounded that a deputy was being attacked. To my dismay, it was the ill-behaving deputy. Apparently, she got into an argument with one of the homosexual inmates who really beat her so badly that she had to be taken to the hospital.

To my surprise, the chief at the time had the audacity to call me to the medical area where the injured deputy was waiting to be taken to the hospital. He tried to blame me for the incident before finding out where I was. Quite angrily, I informed him of my whereabouts and that I couldn't have prevented it. Furthermore, I continued, the deputy had provoked the attack on many levels. First, she didn't know how to speak to the inmates, and second, her behavior did not command their respect. "So, please don't blame me for doing my job. I advised her both on her conduct and language, and she chose to ignore me. Now,

I refuse to be held responsible when I've done my job as a supervisor. And furthermore, I wasn't there to have tried to intervene." I strolled off without awaiting his response. I was already demoted; I had nothing to lose by speaking up for myself and continuing to speak my mind.

Following the attack and her recovery, the deputy was transferred to the front office and never worked the floors again.

Another deputy who was hired after I was flagrantly displayed his macho, male chauvinistic behavior. In fact, I had to ask him several times to leave my floor because he visited the floor when he was not working merely to socialize with the inmates. After he ignored me, I reported him but he was never reprimanded since he was a buddy of Captain Jones who later was promoted to chief and this same deputy was promoted to lieutenant. Both these men had the proud reputation of being womanizers who did as they very well pleased. To prove his point, even after being promoted to lieutenant, he continued to fraternize with the female workers and impregnated one of them, despite his being a married man. Eventually, he went too far.

He had grown so accustomed to getting away with every wrong doing in Fulton County that he expanded his illegal affairs to Alabama County and was caught. I had the satisfaction of seeing him go to jail. Another deputy had previously been caught having sex with a female inmate right there in the jail. The department had become worse than *Peyton Place*.

In the midst of this last storm, I maintained clarity and was aware that I was not the only one being persecuted. All the other deputies who held to high ethical standards were similarly chastised, though none to the extent that I was. It was among them I realized my few friends such as Heidi, Marlena, Fronie, and others.

One male friend was Bryan Turner who finally made lieutenant, after having been passed over several times. Major Riley Taylor, white, was sympathetic toward my situation but there was nothing he could do, not being at the level to intervene and offer a solution. Another friend was Sergeant William Coleman, one of the few decent and non-womanizing males and a pleasure to work and talk with. Our conversations were a buffer to the loneliness that all too often crept over my bones like a spreading sore. I welcomed our commiserations about the administration's unfair treatment of anyone who adhered to

Policy and Procedures. We held fast to the certainty that one day the wrong would be dealt with in God's own way. Or karma's.

*

One final test of my mettle presented itself in the person of Lt. Leyton Graham. I had had two major confrontations with him, the results that bode me ill. The first one involved an altercation between two inmates that ended with one stabbing the other. When Graham investigated the matter, rather than interview me to learn what happened, he merely took the word of a male family member of an inmate, and that family member was not even present at the incident! He then proceeded to verbally censure me. I, in turn, told him bluntly that his investigation was not only unprofessional because it was based upon heresay but disrespectful of me as a female officer. His smug response—that he was the boss and a man, and I was a woman who by this time should know her place—revealed clearly that he had little to no regard for what women had to say.

The second incident was when a female inmate suffered a heart attack while taking a shower and died. Graham proceeded arrogantly and chauvinistically this time to castigate me for negligence. I stoutly pointed out that according to Policy and Procedures, the deputies were *not* supposed to accompany inmates to the bathroom or showers. Furthermore, if the inmate did not complain about feeling ill, the deputies had no way of knowing anything was wrong. It was ridiculous to try to assign blame, especially for a heart attack, which always occurred suddenly.

I raised my voice and exclaimed, "Heart *attack*! Cardiac *arrest*! There's a reason the medical professionals call these incidents by these names. Even while in a hospital and supposedly under professional watch, patients suffer attacks and the staff respond to a Code Blue. And, we are not a hospital. Maybe, you as a man should spend your time implementing a Code Blue system for the jail instead of wasting time bothering people who have other and better things to do."

I had no patience left and certainly no glad sufferance for this fool's pathetic attempt to assert male authority. His smirk, however, warned me that he was awaiting the opportunity to do just that, to show me who the big duck in the little pond was.

His opportunity came upon my retirement. After being demoted a few months prior to my retirement, I was then secretly given back my sergeant status. This meant that when I retired, I should have received the ID badge of a retired lieutenant, similarly to other retirees at my level. Instead, I was given an ID badge of Retired Sergeant and the retirement salary of a Sergeant Deputy. Recognizing that the inequity was intended to persist throughout my retirement, I decided that this last battle was well worth the fight. I'd worked too long and too hard to be shafted. I was off to confront him.

He smirked throughout my explanation then informed me that I should not *even* have gotten the Sergeant ID because I had been *demoted* to Detention Officer. Maintaining my calm, I countered by presenting copies of my pay stubs that designated my Sergeant level. Nonetheless, he said he'd decided to keep my ID and instructed me to write a letter of explanation that detailed what I had just informed on. I did and wrote (replicated here verbatim):

> *Lt. Graham*
> *Fulton County Sheriff Dept.*
> *Office of Professional Standards*
> *185 Central Ave.*
> *Atlanta, Ga. 30303*

Lt. Graham

> *In late October of 2002 I retired from my position as a Fulton County Deputy. Approximately a year or so prior to retiring, I experienced a medical condition that wouldn't allow me to wear a weapon or a gun belt and because of this I had to give up my deputy's position to take a Detention Officers position. In the agreement with Sheriff Barrett, my pay as a Deputy Sergeant did not change and upon my retiring I would receive the same privilege as other Deputy Sergeant's retiring. I should retire at the rank of Lieutenant and receive a badge and ID that indicates such. As you can see, my payroll records indicate that my classification changed back*

> *to Deputy Sergeant just prior to retiring verifying the agreement I had with Sheriff Barrett.*

Respectfully submitted

Maria Pereira

When after a week I received no response, I asked the director of the union, Dennis Hammock, to accompany me. I wanted a first-hand witness of my nemesis's treatment of me, and more important, I simply didn't want to bear the brunt of his vindictiveness and attempts to humiliate me all alone. However, he was a no-show at our appointment and instead left instructions for me to report the matter to Major Antonio Johnson. He in turn advised me to see the sheriff.

Realizing yet another attempt to set me chasing after my own skirt-tail, I dropped the matter. I really didn't need my badge to continue to receive my well-earned, well-deserved pension and its benefits. If denying me my ID badge made Graham feel like a man, let him keep it! His behavior was irrelevant to my peace of mind and good health. All their behavior would recede into the ellipses of life, or otherwise be brought into perspective for contextual reference.

I, on the other hand, will watch how things play out. I'll be a modern-day Esther who looks on while these Hamans are hanged on the gallows they themselves built.

CHAPTER 12 — RIVER OF WATER

I didn't have to wait too long to see my enemies fall. Barrett ran for and won two more terms then abruptly ended her career in law enforcement to disappear like another dried-up river that never made its way to the sea. She had become embroiled in a scheme spearheaded by Byron Rainner, a financial adviser representing New York-based Metropolitan Life Insurance Co. When exposed, it came to light that Rainner had persuaded her to invest up to $7.2 million of jail funds with him. MetLife reimbursed almost all the money, and Rainner pleaded guilty and was sentenced to thirty months in federal prison and ordered to repay a little over two million upon his release. In 2004, Barrett was herself suspended and decided against running for a fourth term. Her career ended in a unerasable public disgrace.

I had some measure of satisfaction in seeing how my intuition regarding Chief Deputy Jones—who had by that time been promoted from Captain—was right all along. I never trusted him from the time he back-stabbed us when we were trying to unionize. Thus, when I read that he, too, was caught in Rainner's con game, I was not surprised and unimpressed by his crocodile tears flowing like a crooked river. A cold-hearted traitor like him was merely using tears to try to manipulate his way into a lesser punishment. I begrudged him, however, that he at least had the decency to surrender due to the part he played. He'd allowed himself to be bribed into selling the Sheriff Office's business for a measly ten thousand dollars. In 2006, he was off to prison. Another public spectacle of shame and disgrace.

The only ones I had empathy for were their respective family members, the true victims of power-trippers and con-artists. How well I recalled how I felt upon learning that I was married to one. But I was young and unwise to the ways of the world. These people were much more mature and ought to have known better. What was their excuse?

Dante has a place in hell for those who become embroiled in the buying and selling of public offices and services. He called them "barrators" whose punishment was submersion in fiery hot pitch from which they could not escape because they were guarded by a horrific demon. If only the punishment that Dante envisioned were true it would be quite a just and fitting one.

*

Sometimes, I didn't feel that I was especially singled out for persecution. I was aware that in my seventeen years in the F.C. Jail I'd never seen any minority immigrant—Caribbean, Latin America, Africa—promoted to the rank of Captain. Obviously, quite a few of us "the foreigners," as we were provincially called, could have done an excellent job if given the opportunity.

When I worked in the Commissary, I'd observed money being misappropriated and the books being audited but no exceptions highlighted. Deputy Noel Blake was a Jamaican who had experience running a facility in New York. He offered to run the Commissary toward improving the department's cost-effectiveness. No one gave him a chance.

There were qualified military men who could have managed the jail so very efficiently, but they too were ignored. For example, a retired colonel of the U.S. Navy was a part of our staff. However, his credentials and experience so intimidated those in leadership—especially the fact that he commanded hundreds of the efficiently trained and ordered—that he was assigned to the kitchen to oversee the trustees. What an insult to his qualifications! In contrast, a female African American deputy with poor vocabulary skills and who cursed like a sailor, and kept six-packs in the trunk of her car was promoted to major. She downed a can of beer immediately upon getting off work; she had to have one for the road; she was promoted to major. I dared to console myself that someone else must have been humiliated or persecuted worse than I was. Those were times when bad politics surely created an environment of very low morale and hostility that cowed most into silence. Maybe, I should have been like them and held my piece. But how could I have? It was in my genes to speak out. Ma did. Grannie did. Most likely, her mother did, too.

So many rivers have disappeared without finding their way to the sea; I dared not be another one.

Now here I am and still determined to have my say, refusing to let what happened silence me yet not quite sure why God allowed me to suffer this persecution, for it was persecution to be demoted only because I spoke out against things that had to exposed. And since I believe that as a child of God everything happened for my own good, I try to make sense of it all from various perspectives.

Some mornings following a refreshing quiet time of bible reading, prayer, and meditation I feel like my persecution was linked to a spiritual war and God alone knows its outcome.

The other morning, I completed my quiet time and wasn't so sure about anything and ended up ranting and raving and asking why me. Especially since like the average person I liked the fairy-tale ending. And if not the happily-ever-after one, well, dammit, give me American justice. I deserved my day in court to argue in my own defense that I was cheated, robbed, and made to look like a fool for doing my job. For refusing to play ball. For doing the right thing. "So why the hell ME?" I shouted to heaven. "Why Mc?! Me? Me?" Calming myself down, I continued in a whisper, "Forgive me, Lord, for my momentary relapse. But you understand, Lord, don't you?"

To console myself, I recalled that when I finally walked away I did so with all the dignity and integrity I could muster and left a legacy that I can be proud of. I'd helped to organize a union that served and protected everyone's interests to this day. I'd serve as its Co-President, Chief Steward, Parliamentarian, President, and Secretary. My track-record on the job was equally exemplary. Noone could deny any of that. I had the satisfaction of knowing that I'd served well at my job. For that, I could continue to face my daughter, two grandchildren, nieces and nephews, and the world with poise and confidence that I'd followed my conscience. I could look back at my tenure and see all the good I'd accomplished and that maybe I could have done some things differently. With a bit more Christian maturity I catalog the maybes:

- Maybe, I wouldn't see everything so strictly as black or white. Right or wrong. People had a right to have a different perspective of things.

- Maybe, I would recognize the grey areas in which people lived and afford them their own canvases on which to paint their shades of grey.

- Maybe, with a better understanding of the spirit of God's law that was more generous than the letter of the law, I would remember that people simply want to be happy and pursue happiness sometimes blindly and counter-productively. Surely, they knew the rules and needed only kind reminders more so than reminders that put them on the defensive.

- Maybe, without having the big picture, I could rest assured that the One who did needed our assistance only to the extent of being Her representation of life and love. I know this idea of God as She is not the typical Christian one; however, I'm no typical Christian—an East Indian Triniboganian, born to a Muslim mother and father (I think he was Muslim), and meandered my way the Creator of all things and everyone.

- So maybe, just maybe, Creator allowed me to walk through fires and swim through rough waters so I could understand me, just me, a little better. Passionate about what I believe and upsetting others along the way. What can I say?

- Maybe — who knows?

*

I had a dream recently. A new sheriff had come to town wearing a new uniform. The only way I recognized her as a sheriff was the hat, the only part of the uniform that hadn't changed. Instead of the brown and beige colors of F.C. department, she wore the vibrant colors of the tropics: bright red blouse, deep mauve skirt, and the mismatched hat in brown. I saw her reviewing my HR files and shaking her head sadly as she read my letter of demotion then cried.

The dream then changed and it was Ma who was weeping silently and telling me to remember that when you dreamt of crying that was a good sign. Then she hugged me, smiled and disappeared into a soft, yellow light before I could ask her what she meant and who the new sheriff was.

I awoke from that dream thinking how strange the dream within a dream was, and how I could always trust anything that Ma said. Always believe all her stories of rivers and mothers who danced upon the waves.

I will continue to be like a tree planted by rivers of water that bring forth fruit in due season—.

GLOSSARY OF CARIBBEAN FOODS

Note: all definitions are taken from the *Dictionary of Caribbean English Usage*, edited by Richard Allsop.

accra (ackra): *n.* a fritter made of shredded saltfish mixed in a batter of flour and seasoning.

bara: *n.* an East Indian patty a few inches in diameter, made from a dough of wheaten flour, ground split peas and turmeric, deep-fried in oil.

callaloo (calalu): *n.* any number of plants with edible, succulent leaves which are cooked as green vegetables.

channa: *n.* chick pea, fried with salt, or boiled and seasoned, served as an inexpensive snack.

doubles: *n.* a type of sandwich made of two BARA with a filling of curried channa, popularly sold as a snack.

mauby: *n.* the bitter-tasting bark of the tree from which a refreshing, non-alcoholic, folk drink is made by fermenting or boiling the bark.

palo(w)ri (-balls)/phulouri(e): small, round balls made of a highly seasoned mixture of ground split-peas and flour, deep fried.

pelau (peleau): *n.* a one-pot meal of rice boiled with pieces of various meats to which pigeon-peas and chipped vegetables are often added; it is sometimes cooked in coconut milk.

pomme-cythere (ponmsitè) [golden apple]: *n.* a solid, roundish fruit with a tough, slightly veined skin which is gold-yellow when ripe; it has a form, acid-sweet, yellow flesh surrounding its spiny seed; this fruit is borne in clusters on a medium-sized tree. [The name is probably derived from its colour and size which make it easily associated with the 'golden apple' of Greek mythology.]

roti: *n.* a kind of unleavened bread made of flour, salt, and water, the dough being rolled flat into thin discs, each baked separately on a baking iron; it is then used to wrap a serving of curry.

sorrel: *n.* a much branched shrub that can grow to about 6 feet, with numerous deeply lobed, light-green leaves and many red-centered, rose-like flowers the calyxes of which develop into deep red, fleshy cups (the fruit), which cover hairy, green seed-pods; the plant dies after one full bearing. The red drink is made from a decoction of these fruit, sometimes called sorrel-drink.

toulum (tooloom, toolum, tulum): *n.* a small round, hard, black cake made of grated coconut, molasses, and sugar; it is much prized as a sweet.

WORKS CONSULTED AND CITED

Ali, Ayaan Hirsi. *Infidel*. New York: Free Press, 2007.

Allette, Bert. "Trini Visiting with Ellie is Atlanta's Deputy Sheriff." *Newsday*. 5 Nov. 2000. P. 35.

Allsopp, Richard, ed. *Dictionary of Caribbean Usage*. Oxford, New York: Oxford UP, 1996.

Alvarez, Julia. *In the Time of the Butterflies*. New York: Penguin Group, 1995.

America's Most Wanted. FoxNews. 9 Nov. 1991.

Clarke, LeRoy. *Douens*. Brooklyn, New York: KaRaEle, 1981.

Cook, Rhonda. "Tearful Ex-Chief Deputy Sentenced." *The Atlanta Journal and the Atlanta Constitution*. 9 Aug. 2007. B3.

Dunn, Julie. "The Ganges." 27 Jul. 2008.

<http://www.csuchico.edu/~cheinz/syllabi/asst001/spring98/ganges.htm>.

Eckstein, Sandra. "Sheriff's Deputies Push for Same Pay as Police." *The Atlanta Journal and the Atlanta Constitution*. 14 Jan. 1999. JH13.

Editorial. "Sergeant Maria Pereira." *International Association of Women Police* (Spring 2004).

Foucault, Michel. *Discipline and Punish: The Birth of the Prison*. New York: Vintage Books, 1979.

Freire, Paulo. *Pedagogy of the Oppressed.*1970. New Revised 20th-anniversary Edition. Trans. Myra Bergman Ramos. New York: Continuum, 1995.

Gaines, Patrice. *Laughing in the Dark: From Colored Girl to Woman of Color: A Journey from Prison to Power*. New York: Doubleday, 1995.

Guisepi, R. A. Ed. "A history of the Ancient Indus River Valley Civilizations." *International World History Project: World History From The Pre-Sumerian Period To The Present*. 27. Jul. 2008 and 02 Jan. 2009. <http://history-world.org/indus_valley.htm>; <http://history-world.org/mainmenu.htm>.

Jackson, George. *Soledad Brother: The Prison Letters of George Jackson*. 1970. Chicago: Lawrence Hill Books, 1994.

James, Joy. *Resisting State Violence: Radicalism, Gender, & Race in U. S. Culture*. Minneapolis and London: U of Minnesota P, 1996.

Johnson, Lara. "Prison Labor: Slavery, Profits and the State." 30 Mar. 1999.

<http://www.prisonactivist.org/Prison-Labor-slavery-profits-and.html.>

Joseph, Francis. "Flying Squad Members Offer Help to Fight Crime." *Trinidad Guardian Online*. 30 Nov. 2008. 28 Mar. 2009. <http://guardian.co.tt/news/crime/2008/11/26/flying-squad-members-offer-help-fight-crime>.

---. "A Police Service in a Mess." *Newsday*. Sunday, 2 Dec. 2007. 28 Mar. 2009. <http://www.newsday.co.tt/news/0,69060.html>.

Marshall, Marilyn. "Georgia's Rev. Sherrif: Richard Lankford Finds Joy in Preaching the Gospel and Keeping the Peace." *Ebony*. March 1986. 92-98.

Martí, José. *Inside the Monster: Writings on the United States and American Imperialism.* Trans. Elinor Randall. New York and London: Monthly Review Press, 1975.

Memmi, Albert. *The Colonizer and the Colonized.* Trans. Howard Greenfeld. Boston: Beacon Press, 1991.

Morrison, Toni. *Song of Solomon.* 1997. New York: Vintage International, 2004.

"Not a Minute More: A Call to the World to End Violence Against Women." The United Nations Development Fund for Women (UNIFEM). 23 Dec. 2002. <http://www.undp.org/unifem/newsroom/events/november_25th.html>.

Nurse, A. Myrna. *Unheard Voices: The Rise of Steelband and Calypso in the Caribbean and North America.* Lincoln, New York, and Shanghai: iUniverse, 2007.

Schlosser, Eric. "The Prison-Industrial Complex." The Atlantic Monthly 282, 6 Dec. 1998: 51-77.

Spivak, Gayatri Chakravorty. *In Other Worlds: Essays in Cultural Politics.* New York and London: Routledge, 1988.

Stanton, Elizabeth Cady. *The Woman's Bible.* 1895. Boston: Northeastern UP, 1993.

Taylor, Quintard. "Jacqueline Barrett." *An Online Reference Guide to African American History.* 30 Dec. 2008. <http://www.blackpast.org/?q=aah/barrett-jacqueline-harrison-1940>.

To the Contrary. "Women in Harm's Way." PBS. Maryland Public Television. 21 May 1993.

"Trinidad and Tobago-National Security." <http://www.photius.com/countries/trinidad_and_tobago/military/national_security.html>.

Williams, Patricia. *The Alchemy of Race and Rights.* Cambridge, MA: Harvard UP, 1991.

ACKNOWLEDGMENTS

This book is dedicated to my loving daughter, **Lynn C. Wong**, and grandchildren, **Kim Marie Wong** and **Jimmy Lee Wong**.

I would also like to thank **Bishop Richard B. Lankford**, former Sheriff of Fulton County for his help in making me fulfill my dreams. My special thank to **Dennis Hammock**, director of International Brotherhood of Police Officers. He has been my friend and loyal supporter through all my problems and has faithfully stood with me throughout the years.

I am also grateful to **Florine Grimes** and **Sergeant Charles Rambo** for having constantly defended my dozens of grievances filed to effect change. To the deputies of integrity whom I am proud to call friends I also owe a debt of gratitude: **Lt. Bryan Turner, Sergeant Fronie Buffington, Sergeant Heidi Schaefer, Deputy Marlena Johnson**, and **Major Cynthia-Dunn-Zachery**.

May God continue to bless you all.

Faithfully,
Maria

*

Myrna thanks the following for their editorial assistance: **Sadayah Lateef** (UG '09, Delaware State University) who, though busy preparing for her graduation, made time to read and offer invaluable suggestions; **Victoria Austin** (UG '10, Delaware State University) for her thoughtful review of the entire manuscript and offering invaluable suggestions toward making Maria's story one of hope; and, **Carolyn Raleigh** (UG '03, University of Delaware) for her attentive rereading of the entire manuscript with the eye of an expert.

Myrna's deepest thanks go to her husband, **Keith**, who continues to lovingly and loyally support and understand the life of an academic, researcher, and writer.

CPSIA information can be obtained
at www.ICGtesting.com
Printed in the USA
FFOW03n1626041215
19217FF